Natural Food Cookery

Natural Food Cookery

by Marya Mavilya

with illustrations by SI FRANKEL

E. A. SEEMANN PUBLISHING, INC.
MIAMI · FLORIDA

*To my husband, Louis,
one of the most outstanding men
in the field of health
and therapy*

"TELL ME WHAT YOU EAT,
AND I WILL TELL YOU WHAT YOU ARE."
—*Brillat-Savarin*

Table of Contents

INTRODUCTION

Only nature can perform the complete life process—the transformation of inorganic substances from out of the earth into organic plants and their eventual consumption by animals and human beings. Unfortunately, "civilization" has, through many generations contributed to the development of today's average man, whose vital chemistry frequently is denatured, deficient and unbalanced. This "feat" modern man has accomplished to a large degree by overcooking the natural food elements in his diet and eating the denatured, devitalized results. This is something that is not to be found in lower creatures regardless of what one element they may eat, for they eat as nature provides.

To revitalize the chemistry of the body, vitally perfect foods will have to be consumed. As the natural properties of foods change through cooking or chemical processes, and the use of heat beyond body temperature destroys food values completely, the process must and should be discarded. My recipes for food—both cold and hot (or, rather, warm)—are rich in true vitamins and their use will give you a body, consistently well, disease-resistant, and therefore beautiful. It will be capable of healing and rebuilding itself and will remain youthfully active throughout its entire life span.

The principal law of life, that LIFE SUSTAINS LIFE, whether in the vegetable or animal kingdom, is strictly adhered to in all of my recipes. The first and most important requisite for good health is the correct use of vital foods.

Those few who know these truths about the urgent importance of correct eating and living are often considered to put it mildly, ODD. While people, in general, are pitifully uninformed where true knowledge is concerned, they are full of firmly implanted, erroneous conceptions that are tremendously difficult to dislodge from their minds, even when these conceptions are obviously distortions of fact.

For instance, we are told that there is nothing more nourishing, more complete as a food than milk. But the processes which the milk that we drink undergoes these days are completely overlooked. Whether pasteurized, homogenized, vitalized or what have you, the vital substances are wholly or partially destroyed. Although some organic chemicals are only partly affected, very few of them can still be used by the blood in its functions. Pasteurization was perhaps imperative when hygienic conditions left much to be desired and the inspection of cows and their attendants was not legally enforced. In removing the danger of infection by germs and bacteria from raw milk, pasteurization destroyed its life and, by extension, that of all milk products: butter, cheese, cream, and ice cream. Therefore, to be a source of vitamins, milk should be consumed "certified raw." It *is* made available to the public in many large cities and some small farm areas as "certified raw."

Take the so-called "staff of life"—bread. To begin

with, the wheat has been so denatured through refining that most of its vital substances have been destroyed. Then it is baked in overheated ovens and the removal of what was left of vital substances is completed.

All the added vitamin pills cannot take the place of the natural ones that have been destroyed.

One can go on and on, through the whole gamut of dishes cooked with excessive heat, canned foods, toasted cereals, vitamin plied flour and milk, which have been robbed of all or almost all of the original vitality, cooked out desserts and candies. These products are so ingeniously advertised that the public is convinced they are *musts* for their growing children. So strong has become the faith in these foods, that natural, raw food is seldom given a thought. In fact, it is often a matter of controversy among our most listened-to nutrition authorities.

The result has been a deplorable deterioration and progressive undermining of the health of American youth. The proof lies bare in a recent government publication which gives startling figures on the number of rejections of our youth for the armed forces. Considering that these "rejects" are our teen-agers, our most select age group, and that the percentage is higher today than it was either in World Wars I or II, there must be something radically wrong. Moreover, this is most typical of America—not other countries. It behooves us to look into it!

My husband remembers how, in the past, working people would take a handful of grain, raw and unprocessed, and use it for their daily bread. Later, they began to use hearth-raised bread which, although still made of the whole natural ingredients, already suffered a partial loss in vitamins because of the heat. But now we eat the standard one pound loaf, baked in an overheated oven.

In his research among the various peoples, my husband found that the matzoth, once a Jewish mainstay, was at one time made of crushed wheat and spring water and then sun dried on the desert sands. It was then a healthful, complete lifegiving food. Today however, even the matzoth has deteriorated and although still an unleavened cracker, it is now baked to a crisp and is hence no longer the useful, invigorating food it once was.

Food is not devitalized when it is air dried, frozen, warmed, smoked, or pickled with natural spices, organic substances, salt and water; nor through transportation, or being gathered unripe. It is devitalized only through excessive heat and chemical processing.

It will help us little to eat a four- to twelve-course dinner, consisting of the best carbohydrates, fats, proteins, minerals, starches, sugars and pill vitamins. After years of eating overcooked and processed foods of the finest quality, the majority of us suffer assorted ailments, which vary from debilitating children's diseases to those of crippled maturity and old age. This state of our health has become accepted as the inevitable pattern of our destiny. Some of us however, will not give in and frequently, hopefully follow new fads in eating and are just as frequently led astray to some degree for a very simple reason: because no matter what foods or combination of them are advocated in these fads, and no matter how excellent the ingredients, they fail if they are cooked or processed to death and thus reduced to working against and not for us.

It is, therefore, not *what* you eat, but *how* it is *prepared*. All foods, as nature produces them, eaten in any combination, are complete, chemically correct and vital, if prepared at body or, at most, at fever heat.

In the recipes that follow, I shall demonstrate the preparation of daily meals which retain all or sufficient vital values and still approach routine or customary eating. For forty-five years my husband has utilized such methods of food preparation. It is our conviction that the whole span of our lives from conception on can be free from all ailments, barring accidents or external infections.

The principles of natural food preparation upon which my husband has based his lifelong work, were instilled in him from his early childhood. The Maviglia (Mavilya) family, of Roman descent, settled several generations ago in agricultural southern Italy-Marcellinara in the province of Calabria. The eating habits of this bountiful farm country were generally correct due to their natural methods of preserving and preparing all types of foods in a variety of ways, e.g.: in olive oil, in salt and water with spices, in salt and water with wine vinegar, in oil and lemon juice, in honey, by air-drying, by salting and low-heat drying, sun drying—always either away from heat or not too close to it. Cheeses were prepared naturally, at below fever temperature. The proverbial Italian wines, which were taken with all of these foods, were merely fermented grapes.

Dr. J. Dudley White, doing so much research on the health and eating habits of peoples around the world, has disclosed the fact that one of the highest degrees of health to be found anywhere in the world can be found in the province of Calabria. My husband came to the same conclusion many years ago when he took his trip around the world for the same purpose. It is the condition in which the food is eaten by these people that plays the major role in keeping them healthy, free from heart ailments, and intestinal distress of any kind.

Depending upon the season of the year, a meal consisted of raw fruits, vegetable salads, one warm course with a blending of one or several of the preserved foods and wine or spring water. The warm course was seared, quickly sizzled or barbecued (as a whole animal), fish or fowl, all done very rare, a sautéed or scalded vegetable, and al dente* spaghetti, macaroni, or noodle dish. At times, a simple meal was composed of slicings of salted, spiced air-dried meats, a fresh salad or combined fresh or naturally preserved combinations of vegetables as a salad, wine, and fresh or sun-dried fruits. When bread was used it was hearth-baked (air-dried in hearth) and of tremendous size—almost as large as King Arthur's round table! It lasted several weeks to a month. Raw and therefore "vital" foods predominated in all meals.

In the course of my husband's research, he came to

---

* *Al dente*—firm to the tooth, water soaked and firm, slightly heated.

know such eminent doctors in New York as Benedict Lust, Will K. Kellogg, and the elder Lindlahr. He learned from them but continued to carry on his own work in accordance with his convictions. He was baffled by the curious fact that so many of his countrymen, who lived on a higher level in America than they had in Italy, were ill. After giving much thought to this phenomenon he decided to make a world-wide survey of human eating habits under various conditions, climatic, social and economic.

He returned, therefore, to the land of his early childhood to compare habits and to discover why healthy Italians became ill in the United States—the land of plenty. He found that although living standards were much higher here so far as housing, conveniences, money and quantities of food were concerned, fundamental principles of living had been thoughtlessly altered or discarded altogether. He saw almost at once that the reasons lay in the destruction of foods by "modern" methods of processing.

In America there were excellent facilities for cooking with more intense and consistent heat than in Italy. Mr. Mavilya made tests in which he compared foods as they were habitually prepared in Italy with those cooked in the United States. The results showed that in Italy less intense heat and less heat or cooking time is used than in this country, and that raw foods, whether fresh or naturally preserved, dominated the daily meals there.

The physique of the people in his little home town had all of the characteristics of good health and vigor, even those in their eighties and nineties. They all had ex-

17

ceptionally fine eyes, good teeth and clear skin. Mr. Mavilya also took into account that apart from the difference in the foods that they consumed, they lived a more outdoor life and consequently had the added benefits of good air and sunshine. They indulged in more physical activity—motion, one of the principal laws of life.

In France and Spain he found food habits similar to those in Italy. In England, Russia and Germany however, he noted that, although the people gave the impression of strength because of their height and robust appearance, they generally had weak eyes, poor teeth and poor digestion. They ate hot, "well-cooked" foods. He realized, of course, that the rigors of the climate in these countries prompted them to warm up with hot foods. Yet, even in these countries in rural communities, where the diet was still simple, people ate much raw food and were consequently healthier than in the cities.

Journeys into Africa, among natives living in the most primitive way, further supported Mr. Mavilya's theories. There, an almost consistent raw food diet prevails and, despite the ills caused by unhygienic conditions, a far healthier physical state exists than in modern "civilized" northern and coastal areas of the world. The conditions that he found among the peoples of India, China, Australia, and South America further confirmed his conclusions that illness was primarily due to incorrect *preparation of* foods, rather than to the *kinds of* foods consumed. He also found that hygienic conditions came second and climatic third—in their influence on health.

Mr. Mavilya determined to teach American men and women how to eat. He began his work among a few people and then, encouraged by the fine results, he decided to aid the many by establishing a health center as a means of spreading his findings and his knowledge.

He has practiced in New York, Connecticut, New Jersey and now in Florida where hundreds of very sick people are brought to better health every year.

We have not yet been able to enjoy the full benefits of our improved *external hygiene* and our bounteous way of living, because we still suffer from the *unhygienic internal* waste which we store up from the devitalized elements in our food intake. We accumulate this waste in our intestines, carry it along in our blood stream, deposit it generally in our tissue cells and alimentary channels. It becomes then the primary basis for many human diseases. Not only can you correct and eliminate disease, but you can prevent it from developing merely by being an intelligent provider of nature's "living" foods.

The Fountain of Youth, so adventurously sought for by Ponce de Leon is indeed within each one of us. We need only know how to taste of it.

Marya Mavilya
Miami Beach, Florida

Natural
Food
Cookery

1. APPETIZERS

FRESH TOMATO JUICE

8 large fresh tomatoes, ripe
1 stalk celery
1 teaspoon coarse salt or sea salt
1 tablespoon onion
½ lime (or lemon), juiced

The vital vitamins and minerals, especially vitamins A, B, and C, abound in this drink. The water soluble quality of vitamin B makes this juice a valuable cache of important values. The A vitamin as a provitamin can be converted and stored in the body.

23

Cut up the tomatoes, mince celery and onion fine, and, along with the balance of ingredients, mix in an electric mixer. Chill.

SAUERKRAUT JUICE

3 lb. head of cabbage
1 tablespoon coarse salt
   or sea salt
1 or 2 lemons, juiced

Low in calories, high in vitamin C and minerals. Keeps small blood vessels strong. Helps strengthen nervous systems. (Magnesium and iron.) Good source of vitamin C so beneficial for gums.

Grate the cabbage and combine with the salt and lemon juice. Place in earthenware jar and press down with a clean stone. Cover and let contents ferment for about two weeks. Use the juice for cocktails and the bulk for sauerkraut.

FRESH SAUERKRAUT WITH FRESH TOMATO JUICE

Chill sauerkraut juice, as made above, and blend with fresh tomato juice. Garnish with lemon or lime peel, as desired.

24

FRESH CRANBERRY JUICE

6 cups fresh cranberries,
  crushed
1 cup honey
Dash of coarse salt
1 teaspoon lemon juice

A source of vitamins A and C. Rich in ascorbic acid. Strengthens small blood vessels, helps to heal bruises, prevent bleeding gums.

Crush the cranberries, or put into blender. Mix with honey. Dilute with water or orange juice to taste, and garnish with fresh peppermint leaves. Serve chilled or with ice.

APRICOT AND OTHER DRIED FRUIT JUICE

½ lb. dried apricots,
  natural unsulphured
3 to 4 cups water
½ cup honey
1 drop of peppermint
  oil, or 1 teaspoon
  fresh peppermint, or
  a pinch dried pepper-
  mint leaves

Tremendous amount of vitamin A, so can aid in keeping the skin in good condition. Can avoid "gooseflesh" type of skin disorder. The eyes are benefited, too.

Combine the ingredients with the water and soak over-overnight. Put into an electric blender and liquify. Chill. Prepare PRUNES, FIGS, PEACHES, and other dried fruits in this same way.

25

MELON BALLS IN SAUTERNE WINE

3 cups watermelon, cantaloupe or, honey-dew melon balls
1 cup natural unsweet-ened Sauterne wine
½ cup honey
1 tablespoon lemon juice

Calories low and vitamins A and C high. Makes skin flourish with healthful appearance and corrects skin blemishes. Mineral salts aid in cleansing the kidneys.

Blend honey with wine and pour over melon balls in individual glasses and serve chilled. Peppermint leaves may be added for color and flavor.

BERRY-MINT COCKTAIL

Use strawberries or fresh raspberries
Honey, to taste
Lemon juice, to taste
Fresh chopped pepper-mint leaves

The tastiness and eye appeal here are great. Vitamins A and C help keep small blood vessels strong and firm. Mint leaves are a source of chlorophyll and have neutralizing effect on biliousness and stomach upsets.

Wash and hull berries, combine with honey to taste and fresh peppermint leaves. Serve chilled in individual sherbet dishes.

26

STUFFED CANTALOUPE HALVES

Chilled cantaloupes
Bananas
Certified raw cream or
   fresh coconut milk
Honey, to taste

Aids in the prevention of night blindness. Rich in vitamin C good for small blood vessels, gums, and healing. Contains nourishing, energy-giving vegetable protein.

Cut cantaloupes into halves and slice bananas into them. Add certified raw cream or, even better, the fresh coconut milk.

BACON AND CHEESE MORSEL

Lean bacon, Canadian
   style
Natural blue cheese or
   aged Cheddar, sliced
   into one-inch pieces

High in protein, phosphorus.

Cut bacon into two-inch strips. Wrap a strip of bacon around each piece of cheese and fasten with a toothpick.

COCONUT JUICE COCKTAIL

1 fresh coconut
Water of coconut

Rich source of B-vitamins and high in mineral values, especially phosphorus. As a potent protein, it supplies high energy, and promotes bone building. Frequently used as a milk for children.

Place both coconut water and cut-up coconut meat in an electric mixer. Can be combined successfully with almost any fruit: cherries, strawberries, bananas, and pineapple are very delectable. Add water as desired. A bit of honey may be used.

FRESH APPLE JUICE *

Fresh Apples
Water
Honey, if desired
Lemon juice, if desired

Outstanding in vitamin A, necessary for membranes of eyes and to help prevent night blindness. The pectin in apples aids in treating diarrhea. "An apple a day" can be stored in the body for general health purposes.

* Fresh peaches, apricots, pears and similar fruits can be handled in the same way for juice or sauce.

To extract the juice of apples, grate them or put them into an electric mixer, starting the juicing with a little water. Add honey and lemon juice. The bulk makes an excellent apple sauce. Serve chilled.

FRESH GRAPE JUICE

6 lbs. grapes
1 cup honey
1 lemon, juiced
Water

A vital deposit of vitamins A and C, minerals such as iron and natural sugar. Few calories. Ascorbic acid keeps blood vessels strong and well formed.

Pick grapes off stems, combine with honey to taste, lemon juice, and water and mix in an electric mixer until liquid. Served chilled.

FRESH VEGETABLE JUICE

4 stalks celery
6 carrots, grated
2 parsley clusters
4 tomatoes, red ripe
2 cucumbers
½ cup water
¼ teaspoon coarse salt
⅛ teaspoon crushed red pepper, if desired

Retain all skins; source of fragile vitamin C is on the outside. High in calcium and phosphorus (for building teeth and bones), it serves well for pregnant mothers.

29

Mix all ingredients in an electric mixer with water and seasonings. Chill before serving. Other combinations that appeal to individual tastes can be evolved to make delicious cocktails. When using carrots in an electric blender, cut them into slices or shred.

FRUIT CUP MEDLEY

2 oranges, cut
1 grapefruit, cut
2 apples, cut
3 bananas, cut
1 cup fresh berries in season
½ cup orange juice
Honey to taste

Provides complete assortment of vitamins A, B and C, and the minerals necessary for body growth and vigor.

Mix together and serve in a chilled sherbet glass. Add some Sauterne wine, if you wish. Serves 6 to 8.

BANANA COCKTAIL

1 cup fresh orange juice
½ cup fresh grapefruit juice
4 bananas, diced or sliced
Honey to taste

A complete food. Energizing, rich in natural sugar. Used by some diabetics.

Mix all ingredients and serve chilled.

FRESH PEACH IN PORT WINE

2 large fresh peaches,
   sliced
½ cup honey
1 cup natural port wine

Stimulating and rich in vital minerals, especially iron.

Blend honey with wine and pour over peaches in individual glasses and serve chilled.

NO-COOK "DIPS" AND "BITS"

BLUE CHEESE-WIN

¼ lb. blue cheese
2 tablespoons dry red
   wine
Celery or cucumber slices

Cheese is highest in protein value, next to meats. It promotes growth and maintains nitrogen equilibrium. The dietary fat content is good for skin, and, according to some authorities, for reproductive function.

Mix together the cheese and wine until creamy and serve on celery bits (cut into 1" or 2" inch pieces), or on slices of cucumber.

MUSHROOM CHEESE BLEND

¼ lb. fresh small white mushrooms
1 lb. cottage cheese or Camembert cheese
1 teaspoon grated lemon rind
Celery or cucumber slices

Calorie sum low in mushrooms, yet they are rich in calcium, copper, and vitamins A, B and C. Aids in preventing diarrhea.

Chop the mushrooms very fine. Blend with cheese and lemon rind. Serve on celery bits or slices of cucumber.

RAW PEANUT BUTTER BALLS

1 cup raw peanut butter
1½ cups raw peanuts, finely crushed
Dash coarse salt

Surplus of B vitamins here. Raw peanuts are a complete protein and often used, liquefied with water and honey, as a substitute for milk. Nuts are efficiency experts for physical and mental fitness.

Soften the raw peanut butter by mixing with salt and then form into small balls. Roll in crushed raw peanuts and serve as such or with colorful toothpicks.

VEGETABLE SKEWERS

1 cup small white
   onions
2 firm tomatoes, or 12
   small cherry toma-
   toes
1 stalk celery, cut into
   one-inch pieces
1 green pepper, cut into
   squares
1 cucumber, sliced
¼ lb. fresh small white
   mushrooms
6 small white potatoes

Vitamins A, B and C plus min-
erals, on a stick. Good for growth
in the young, and for repair in the
adult.

Use small four-inch wooden skewers and arrange the vegetables in any order to make them attractive. The onions
may be pickled.

SOUR CREAM ONION ZIP

1 cup sour cream
1 green scallion,
   chopped fine
3 fresh red radishes,
   chopped or sliced fine
1 small cucumber, sliced
   fine

Plenty of vitamins A, B, and C
as well as calcium, phosphorus
and iron here. In fermentation,
such as soured cream and other
soured milk products, one finds

1 stalk green leaves of
   celery
Coarse salt and black
   ground pepper

elements that are potent growth factors. They also help in overcoming lassitude.

Combine sour cream with one chopped scallion, radishes, and other vegetables; add seasonings. Serve on celery bits, cucumber slices, raw beet slices, green pepper quarters, or scooped out tomato wedges. For variation, add chopped green pepper or mushrooms to the cream.

CHEESE BALLS

¼ lb. blue cheese
 1 cup chopped walnuts,
   pecans, almonds or
   raw peanuts

Good blend of protein and carbohydrates. Nuts are important as a vegetable source of fat—necessary for body function, especially under skin and for protection around kidneys and other organs.

Roll balls out of blue cheese and cover completely with finely chopped or crushed nuts. Put colorful toothpicks in balls and serve.

MINIATURE SHISH KEBOB

½ lb. sirloin of lamb or
   beef

1 tablespoon yogurt
½ teaspoon ginger
¼ teaspoon minced onion
1 teaspoon poppy seed
1 clove garlic, minced
Coarse salt and pepper
Salad oil, corn or olive
1 green pepper
¼ lb. white small mushrooms
6 small potatoes
8-10 small cherry tomatoes
8 small white onions

Meat—the full protein for building up the body and its strength. Accompanying vegetables provide additional vitamins and minerals for increased energy.

Cut the meat into 1-inch squares. Cover meat with marinade made of yogurt and all ingredients except vegetables. Marinate for about an hour. (Use a lemon, juiced, if desired.) Thread the meat on skewers along with the vegetables. Brush with oil and heat over high flame for about 2 to 4 minutes.

STUFFED ZUCCHINI

1 lb. zucchini
3 tablespoons finely chopped onion
¼ cup chopped almonds

Vitamin A to safeguard skin and eyes. Nuts for body-building protein.

35

½ teaspoon finely
chopped parsley

4 tablespoons sour
cream or Ricotta
cheese

½ lemon, juiced

2 tablespoons butter

Scrub the squash well; halve lengthwise and cut into 2-inch pieces. Scoop out the interior, leaving the shell. Chop the meat of the zucchini and combine with onion, parsley, and butter. Quickly sear and then mix with the remaining ingredients and stuff into squash shells. Sprinkle with parsley.

2. SOUPS

TOMATO

6 ripe tomatoes
1 tablespoon grated
   onion or scallion
2 cups water
Dash of oregano
1 basil leaf
3 tablespoons olive oil
Coarse salt and red
   crushed pepper, as de-
   sired

Since B vitamins are water soluble, soups are valuable reservoirs of the vegetable elements. Vitamin B tomatoes help keep the small blood vessels and gum tissue firm.

Liquefy the tomatoes in an electric mixer. Add onion and seasonings, then water. *WARM, DO NOT COOK!*

SOUPS

VEGETABLE

3 cups liquefied toma-
 toes (fresh)
1 carrot grated
1 cup fresh green peas,
 or frozen peas
½ cup raw potato, diced
1 stalk celery leaves
2 tablespoons chopped
 parsley
1 green pepper, diced
1 basil leaf
1 teaspoon oregano
3 tablespoons olive oil
½ cup raw oatmeal
1 or 2 cups water
½ teaspoon coarse salt
 and red crushed pep-
 per, as desired

No vitamin shortage here!

Heat the liquefied tomatoes with water; add oil, vegetables, and seasonings. At the very end of warming, mix
in the raw oatmeal. This provides a bit of thickening and
excellent flavor. Keep stirring over heat until hot. (3 to
5 minutes)

MINESTRONE

6 fresh ripe tomatoes
2 scallions, chopped
1 green pepper, diced

The Italian flair in soup.

2 stalks celery, cut up
  with leaves
Dash oregano
1 basil leaf
½ teaspoon coarse salt
  and ¼ teaspoon red
  crushed pepper
3 tablespoons olive oil
1 or 2 cups hot water
Spaghettini, fine noodles
  or little bits of maca-
  roni

Sear very quickly the scallions, green pepper, and celery leaves in 1 tablespoon olive oil. Combine all of these vegetables with the noodles, seasonings, oil, and hot water. Heat until hot, *careful not to cook*. May be served with grated cheese, Parmesan type. Soak the noodles in hot water with salt for about five minutes.

POTATO SOUP

2 cups raw new pota-
  toes, diced
1 onion, chopped
2 tablespoons butter or
  olive oil
1 celery stalk, chopped
1 or 2 cups water or raw
  certified milk
Coarse salt and pepper,
  as desired

Don't peel skins where the perishable vitamin C is stored. The salts in potatoes help enrich blood, and prevent emaciation and diarrhea.

39

Sear onion, potatoes, and celery in oil or butter. Add the water and seasonings. Put all ingredients in the electric blender and liquefy. Just *warm* and serve.

CHICKEN SOUP

4 cups chicken soup stock, or chicken powder or bouillon
1 carrot, grated
1 onion, grated
1 stalk celery leaves, minced
1 bay leaf
1 basil leaf
1 sprig of parsley
Coarse salt and pepper, as desired

Mineral values here and the added vegetables combine to make this rich in vitamins A, B and C. Both body and energy building. A treat for the palate.

Make chicken stock out of wings, neck, and entrails by simmering together with onions and celery for about 5 minutes. Strain the liquid stock and add to the raw chopped or liquefied vegetables. Throw away the chicken and the vegetables that have been simmered. *Warm* the chicken stock and add the raw vegetables when about to serve.

GREEN PEA SOUP

2 cups fresh peas in sea-
   son, or fresh frozen
3 cups water
1 scallion, chopped fine
2 slices Canadian bacon
2 tablespoons olive oil
Coarse salt and red
   crushed pepper, as de-
   sired

Phosphorus here, good for bones. Fresh peas are high in Vitamins A, B and C.

Liquefy the green peas with a little water in an electric mixer. Warm in a pan the Canadian bacon. Mix the bacon and its own fat with the olive oil and the scallion and heat the entire mixture with the liquefied peas. Add water until you reach desired thickness. Add seasonings to taste.

CORN CHOWDER

2 cups whole kernel corn
   (cut from raw ears of
   corn)
1 small potato, grated
1 small onion, grated
1 small green pepper,
   diced including seeds
3 cups certified raw milk
3 tablespoons olive oil
Coarse salt and red
   crushed pepper

The kernels and seeds are an excellent source of B vitamins.

Sear the potato, onion, and green pepper one minute in olive oil. Liquefy in an electric blender. Add the corn and other ingredients and warm for about 3 minutes. Serve.

CREAMED MUSHROOM SOUP

¼ lb. fresh mushrooms, sliced
1 small scallion, chopped
3 cups certified raw milk
3 tablespoons olive oil
3 tablespoons whole wheat or rice flour
Coarse salt and pepper, as desired

The mushroom, long overlooked and cast aside as merely an added garnish is now recognized as a source of B vitamin. Mushrooms must grow in rich soil and are therefore full of iodine as well.

Sauté the scallion quickly in oil over high heat. Add the fresh mushrooms when pan is removed from the fire. Add the milk and put into an electric blender until mushrooms and scallion are liquefied. Heat and stir constantly until hot. Add the seasonings, flour, and oil and serve.

FISH CHOWDER

1 cup shredded raw white fish
1 scallion, chopped
1 cup raw diced potato

Minerals needed for healthy bones and teeth. Source of Vitamin D,

1 stalk celery, chopped
1 cup mashed fresh to-
matoes
½ cup fresh green pep-
per, minced
3 tablespoons olive oil
Coarse salt and pepper,
as desired
Dash oregano
2 cups water

so important for pregnant women. Oil is rich in D which is hard to find in foods. (Sunshine best source.)

Sear rapidly for 1 minute onion, potato, celery, and peppers in olive oil. When pan is removed from heat, add the tomatoes and corn. Warm the fish in water and seasonings. Combine the seared vegetables with fish broth. Serve with grated cheese if desired.

SPLIT PEA SOUP

1 cup split peas
1 tablespoon coarse
salt
3 cups water
1 onion grated
1 bay leaf
1 basil leaf
½ teaspoon oregano
Smoked ham bone
Coarse salt and pepper,
as desired

High quantities of phosphorus for strong bones.

43

SOUPS

Soak peas in water with one tablespoon salt for 48 hours or until soft. Make ham stock out of ham bone and water by simmering together for about five minutes. Let stand for a half hour. Drain the water off the split peas and add them to the warmed ham stock. Put half of the split peas and the onion and seasonings into an electric blender to liquefy them. They will make the soup thicker, and easier to digest. Heat until hot, constantly stirring.

3. VEGETABLES

ASPARAGUS SAUTÉ

2 cups fresh asparagus
1 teaspoon grated onion
 or 1 garlic clove
2 tablespoons olive or
 peanut oil
Coarse salt and coarse
 black pepper, as de-
 sired

Vitamins A, B and C, as well as calcium, phosphorus, iron and other minerals are found here. These vitamins make the neces- sary co-enzymes that control the important enzyme-controlled re- action, that establishes good health. The eyes are aided by the large amount of Vitamin A here.

Break asparagus into pieces 2 inches long, place in sauce- pan with oil, season. Add garlic section or grated onion and warm quickly over low heat for about two minutes.

45

Keep turning pieces over and over in pan. Serve in a covered casserole.

ASPARAGUS CHEESE VARIATION

Follow recipe for Asparagus Sauté above, and add grated Parmesan or Romano type cheese

The added protein in cheese is a growth factor and protector for body health.

Mix all ingredients thoroughly and turn into casserole dish to serve, sprinkling more cheese on the top.

WINED ASPARAGUS

2 cups fresh asparagus
2 tablespoons olive oil
1 teaspoon wine vinegar or lemon juice
1 tablespoon white Sauterne wine
1 teaspoon honey

Stimulating wine and natural sugar round out this food as a wholesome energy builder.

Break asparagus into pieces two inches long, place in saucepan with oil and warm quickly for about two minutes, turning pieces over and over. Mix wine vinegar, Sauterne wine, and honey thoroughly and pour over asparagus just before serving.

ARTICHOKES

4 whole artichokes,
  small
4 tablespoons olive oil
1 small onion, grated
½ cup water
Coarse salt and coarse
  black pepper, as de-
  sired

Chlorophyll plus innumerable vitamins and minerals make this a valuable as well as challenging vegetable. The natural sugar is recommended for quick energy.

Heat water, season, and place artichokes sprinkled with oil in pan containing water and onion. Sizzle for five minutes using very low heat. Remove from heat keeping cover on for another minute.

DRIED BEANS

2 cups dried beans (red
  kidney, fava, navy
  beans, etc.)
4-6 tablespoons olive oil
2 tablespoons honey
Coarse salt and red
  crushed pepper, as de-
  sired

High in calories, to be sure, but so high in minerals too!

FOR VARIATION:

1 onion, diced
2 stalks celery, diced

47

1 green pepper, diced
Coarse salt and red
   crushed pepper

Soak beans in water 48 hours with 2 tablespoons coarse salt. Change water 4 times. Sear onion, celery and green pepper quickly over high heat in frying pan with oil. Combine with the warmed beans and serve in a covered casserole.

LIMA BEAN CONCOCTION

2 cups lima beans
Coarse salt
1 stalk celery with
   leaves, cut up
1 cup raw green peas
4 tablespoons olive oil
Coarse salt and red
   crushed pepper, as de-
   sired

The lima bean can be used either dried or fresh, or frozen. The baby limas are especially high in protein and Vitamins A, B and C. As such, they are of value in growth of bones, teeth and muscle tissue.

Follow recipe for soaking above. Mix with fresh vegetables and serve in casserole as with the recipes above for dried beans.

LIMA BEANS AND FRESH TOMATO COMBINE

2 cups lima beans,
soaked 48 hours
4 fresh tomatoes
1 onion, chopped fine
1 teaspoon honey
4 slices raw lean bacon,
minced
1 tablespoon chopped
parsley
2 tablespoons olive, corn
or peanut oil
Coarse salt and red
crushed pepper, as de-
sired

The combination of tomatoes with its high Vitamin C content converts this dish into a richer ABC and mineral reserve for the body.

Sauté the beans in oil over slow heat, stirring constantly until warm. Add tomatoes, onion, bacon and parsley and continue to saute until all of the vegetables are warm. Add seasoning to taste, and serve in a covered casserole.

CHILE

2 cups red beans
4 tablespoons coarse salt
2 stalks celery, chopped
1 onion, chopped
1 green pepper, diced
4 teaspoons Chile pow-
der

The important bean again. The chile and vegetables convert this into a high Vitamin C product. A dish to aid the vigorous working man.

49

Soak beans 48 hours in salt water, changing it 3 or 4
times. Sear quickly in oil over high flame (2-3 minutes
until hot and firm), the celery, onion and green pepper.
Add the chile powder, salt, and, if desired, 4 crushed tomatoes. In another pan, warm the beans in oil over slow
heat, turning constantly until warm. Blend both mixtures
together and serve in a covered casserole.

BEETS

4 large red beets with
  greens
3 tablespoons olive oil
  or butter
1 teaspoon lemon or
  lime juice
1 teaspoon honey
Coarse salt and coarse
  black pepper, as de-
  sired

*A mine of minerals, especially
iron for blood building.*

Wash and dice beets. Add greens cut into small pieces.
If not desired, the green tops may be omitted. Warm over
slow heat in either oil or butter, turning constantly. Remove from heat and add honey, lemon juice and seasoning.

HARVARD BEETS

2 cups diced or thinly
   sliced raw beets
4 tablespoons honey
¼ cup lemon juice
1 tablespoon Sauterne
   wine
1 tablespoon olive oil
Coarse salt and coarse
   black pepper, as de-
   sired
3 tablespoons water
4 tablespoons whole
   wheat flour

In wheat flour, the iron and niacin (B) for muscle strengthening.

Mix flour with water and warm over low heat, stirring constantly. Add honey, lime or lemon juice, sauterne wine, oil and seasonings. Stir in beets turning constantly over slow heat until they are warm. (3-5 minutes)

GRATED BEETS

2 cups raw beets, grated
2 tablespoons melted
   butter or olive oil
1 teaspoon honey
1 teaspoon lemon or
   lime juice
Coarse salt and coarse
   black pepper, as de-
   sired

The grating of beets provides an easy step in the digestion of this vegetable. Also useful in constipation disorders (use a little at a time because very effective).

51

Mix together beets, butter or oil, honey and lemon juice and warm over slow heat turning over constantly. Add seasoning and serve.

RAW BEETS AND SWEET AND SOUR PICKLE

2 cups raw beets, grated
4 tablespoons pickles, sweet or sour, diced
3 tablespoons honey
1 tablespoon wine vinegar
½ teaspoon coarse salt

An additional amount of Vitamin A for eyes is found here.

Combine all these ingredients, chill and serve.

RAW BEETS AND HORSERADISH

1 cup raw beets, grated
1 cup white hot radish, grated
3 tablespoons cider vinegar
1 teaspoon olive, corn or peanut oil
½ teaspoon coarse salt

Appetizing blood builder.

Combine all ingredients, chill and serve as a relish. The longer it is allowed to marinate the stronger and better.

BROCCOLI

1 bunch of broccoli, cut
  into 1" pieces
4 tablespoons butter or
  olive oil
Coarse salt and red
  crushed pepper, as de-
  sired

A good source of alkaline salts for neutralizing the excess acids in the body.

Wash and cut or chop broccoli, place into saucepan, add butter or oil and seasoning. Use very low heat and turn over frequently until broccoli is warm. For broccoli au gratin add grated Romano or Parmesan cheese.

BRUSSELS SPROUTS IN CHEESE SAUCE

2 cups Brussels sprouts,
  cut fine or ground
½ cup grated Parmesan
  or Romano cheese
1 cup certified raw
  milk
4 tablespoons whole
  wheat flour
Coarse salt and coarse
  black pepper, as de-
  sired

Mostly Vitamin A for the eyes here. Cheese as protein builds bone, muscle tissue and teeth.

Warm milk mildly, add butter, cheese, flour and seasoning, stirring constantly over very low heat. Add sprouts and stir until warm. (3 to 5 minutes)

CABBAGE

3 cups shredded cabbage
4 tablespoons butter or olive oil
Coarse salt and red crushed pepper, as desired

The Vitamin C elevates the cabbage. Eaten raw or slightly warmed as here, it aids in keeping small blood vessels strong and well formed. Shredded, it is easily digested.

With the butter or oil and the seasoning sauté shredded cabbage quickly over low heat, turning over constantly.

SCALDED CABBAGE

1 head of cabbage, cut into four sections
4 tablespoons butter, olive or peanut oil
Coarse salt and red crushed pepper, as desired
Hot water, enough to cover cabbage

Rich in calcium and other minerals, it helps bone building and neutralizes acids in the system.

Place enough water in pot to cover four sections of head of cabbage and heat it to "hot," but *not* boiling. In one minute take cabbage out of water, season and use either butter or oil when serving. Some people like lemon juice, also.

CABBAGE WITH BACON BITS

2 cups shredded cabbage
1 cup chopped raw lean bacon or Canadian bacon
½ cup diced celery
2 tablespoons olive oil
Coarse salt and red crushed pepper, as desired

Bacon adds the dietary fat needed in body and aids in regulating body heat (especially good in winter).

Sauté the vegetables and bacon combined with oil and seasoning quickly over very low heat. (2 to 4 minutes)

SOUR CABBAGE

1 cup shredded cabbage
1 cup shredded cabbage, soaked about 1 hour in 4 tablespoons of sour cider vinegar, or use sauerkraut

A tasty variation of the high mineral properties of cabbage.

2 tablespoons olive oil
Coarse salt and coarse
   black pepper, as de-
   sired

Combine the cabbage with oil and the seasonings. Sauté quickly over very slow heat turning constantly.

CABBAGE AND NUT CONCOCTION

2 cups shredded cab-
   bage
½ cups chopped pecans
   or raw peanuts
3 tablespoons olive or
   peanut oil
Coarse salt and coarse
   black pepper, as de-
   sired

The nuts add Vitamins A and B to the C in the cabbage.

Combine cabbage and nuts, olive or peanut oil and seasonings. Sauté quickly over low heat constantly stirring. (2-4 minutes)

CABBAGE AND CARROTS SAUTÉED

1 cup shredded cab-
   bage
½ cup chopped or
   shredded carrots

Provides natural sugars. Rich in Vitamins A, B and C.

4 tablespoons butter,
   olive or peanut oil
Coarse salt and coarse
   black pepper, as de-
   sired

Combine cabbage and carrots with butter or oil and seasonings, and sauté over low heat, turning slowly and
constantly until warm.

CARROTS

2 cups raw carrots,
   grated
3 tablespoons butter or   *Pure carotene, the absolutely per-*
   olive oil   *fect form of Vitamin A for the*
Coarse salt and coarse   *care of the eyes. A source of nat-*
   black pepper, as de-   *ural sugar. All very beneficial for*
   sired   *the eyes, skin and hair.*

Sauté the carrots in butter or oil and seasonings over a
low heat and stir constantly until warm. (2-4 minutes)

CREAMED CARROTS

2 cups raw carrots,
   diced or grated
1 cup certified raw milk   *Add the protein in milk and*

4 tablespoons whole
wheat flour

3 tablespoons butter or
olive oil

Coarse salt and coarse
black pepper, as de-
sired

butter or oil and here is nutrition personified. The whole wheat flour contains B vitamins.

Combine carrots with milk, flour, butter or oil and season-ings. Stir constantly over very slow heat until warm and a little thickened. (3-5 minutes)

CARROTS AND PEAS

1½ cups raw diced car-
rots

1 cup fresh green peas

1 tablespoon grated
onion, or cut scal-
lion

1 stalk celery, diced

3 tablespoons olive or
peanut oil

Coarse salt and coarse
black pepper, as de-
sired

An old favorite, full of vitamins, especially A. Of chemical value to eyes, skin, hair and blood.

Combine carrots, peas, onion and celery with oil and seasonings, and sauté over low heat turning constantly until warm.

CARROTS AND CELERY

1 cup raw diced carrots
1 cup raw diced celery
1 tablespoon grated
  onions
1 tablespoon chopped
  parsley
1 teaspoon honey
Coarse salt and coarse
  black pepper, as de-
  sired
3 tablespoons creamed
  butter, olive oil
1 cup certified raw milk
4 tablespoons whole
  wheat flour
2 tablespoons butter or
  olive oil

The abundance of Vitamin A in carrots supplements the lack of it in celery. Together they are highly nutritious. Creamed, they are even more protein-rich.

Season and sauté carrots, celery, onion and parsley in honey and butter or oil over slow heat, stirring constantly until warm. To cream the above, warm milk mildly with butter and whole wheat flour and add to the vegetables. (2-4 minutes)

CAULIFLOWER

2 cups cauliflower
3 tablespoons butter or
  olive oil

Vitamins A, B and C and min-

☞

59

Coarse salt and red crushed pepper, as desired

4 tablespoons whole wheat flour, if desired

erals make this an excellent body protector.

Cut cauliflower into small pieces and sauté in butter or oil and seasoning over low heat, turning constantly until warm. ADD the flour if a "breaded" taste is desired. (3-5 minutes)

CAULIFLOWER AU GRATIN

The added protein in cheese makes this a valuable tissue builder.

Using two cups of cauliflower, follow recipe for creaming carrots. (CREAMED CARROTS) For cauliflower au gratin, follow recipe for BRUSSELS SPROUTS WITH CHEESE SAUCE.

CAULIFLOWER AND FRESH MUSHROOMS

1½ cups cauliflower

1 cup diced fresh mushrooms

2 tablespoons whole wheat flour

4 tablespoons butter or olive oil

½ teaspoon coarse salt

Valuable salts and copper and other minerals. High iodine content.

¼ teaspoon red
crushed or black
pepper
Ingredients for creaming,
if desired:
2 tablespoons butter
or olive oil
2 tablespoons whole
wheat flour
1 cup raw certified
milk
Coarse salt and pepper

Sauté cauliflower, flour and seasonings in butter or oil.
Remove from heat, add mushrooms, stir and cover until
mushrooms are warmed. (3-5 minutes)

CELERY

2 cups diced celery
2 tablespoons olive,
corn or peanut oil or
1 cup of water
½ teaspoon coarse salt
¼ teaspoon black pep-
per

Excellent for nerve tissue. Especially recommended for people who do not sleep well, get up tired, are restless, continually fatigued or nervous and jittery.

Sauté celery in oil or water and seasonings over slow heat.
Turn constantly until warm. (2-3 minutes) Celery should
be eaten RAW, as much as possible.

CREAMED CELERY

2 cups diced celery
1 tablespoon butter or
olive oil
1 tablespoon grated
onion
1 cup raw certified milk
3 tablespoons whole
wheat flour
Coarse salt and coarse
black pepper, as de-
sired
¼ cup almonds, minced

Same properties as above. Added milk and butter give a protein plus.

Wash the celery well. Warm the milk slowly over very low heat. Add the flour, oil and seasonings. Add celery and onion when the cream mixture is thick enough; (2-4 minutes). May add minced almonds.

CORN ON COB

4 ears of corn in husks
Coarse salt and pepper
Butter
4 cups water with coarse
salt

Vitamin A and rich phosphorus help eyes, build teeth and bone.

Place corn in covered pot of hot water. Leave 5 minutes. Serve after removing husks, adding butter and seasoning.

CORN SAUTÉED

2 cups raw corn, cut off
  cob
2 tablespoons butter or
  olive oil
1 teaspoon honey
½ green pepper, diced
2 tablespoons chopped
  onion
¼ teaspoon coarse black
  pepper

Protein in butter and milk gives full value to the corn, which is an incomplete protein food.

Combine corn, green pepper, onion, honey and seasonings with butter or oil. Sauté in saucepan and stir constantly over low heat until warm. (2-4 minutes)

OVEN CORN ON COB

Corn may be placed in a very hot oven for about five minutes with the husks on. Add butter and seasonings and serve.

CREAMED CORN KERNELS

2 cups raw corn sliced
  from cob

☞

VEGETABLES

2 tablespoons butter, or
  olive oil
1 cup certified raw milk
3 tablespoons whole
  wheat flour
1 teaspoon honey
1 teaspoon grated onion
2 tablespoons diced
  green pepper
Coarse salt and red
  crushed pepper, as de-
  sired

A complete protein package.

Warm the milk with flour, seasonings and oil or butter. Combine with corn, onion and green pepper in a saucepan, stirring constantly until warm. Use very low heat. (2-4 minutes)

For CORN AU GRATIN:

Add to the Creamed Corn Kernels recipe, grated Parmesan cheese to taste.

SUCCOTASH

1 cup raw corn, cut off
  cob
1 cup raw green lima
  beans
3 tablespoons shredded
  green pepper

Beneficial for general building and rebuilding of body.

1 teaspoon grated
  onion
Butter or oil to taste
Coarse salt and red
  crushed pepper, as de-
  sired

Combine corn, lima beans, green pepper and onion with oil and seasonings. Stir constantly over very low heat until warm. (3-5 minutes)

SAUTÉED EGGPLANT

1 large eggplant, cut into
  1 inch slices with peel
2 tablespoons butter,
  olive, or peanut oil
Coarse salt and red
  crushed pepper, as de-
  sired

Calorie low and vitamin and mineral high. With peel that is a real cache of mineral properties for building bones, teeth and muscle tissue.

Combine eggplant with oil and seasonings, and sauté over low heat, turning slowly and constantly until warm.

EGGPLANT WITH WHOLE WHEAT

1 large eggplant, cut into
1 inch slices with peel

2 tablespoons butter, olive or peanut oil
4 tablespoons whole wheat flour

The B vitamins in whole wheat good for bad nerves.

Follow recipe as indicated for SAUTEED EGGPLANT adding 4 tablespoons whole wheat flour. Dip slices of eggplant in flour and sauté on each side over low flame. (1-2 minutes)

TOMATO EGGPLANT

2 cups cubed eggplant
3 tomatoes, chopped
½ cup diced green pepper
1 stalk diced celery
2 tablespoons olive or peanut oil
Coarse salt and crushed red pepper, as desired

Vitamin C plus rich minerals in eggplant.

Combine eggplant, tomatoes, flour, oil and seasonings. Sauté over low heat, stirring constantly. For variation, add 1 cup raw corn cut off cob.

EGGPLANT AU GRATIN

3 tablespoons grated
   Parmesan cheese
Milk (usually 1 cup, de-
   pending on desired
   thickness)

Highly nutritious in the added protein of cheese and milk. The iron found in eggplant is important for good blood.

Add the cheese and milk to Tomato Eggplant recipe, using 1 tomato instead of 3.

GREEN BEANS

1 or 2 cups green beans,
   cut in French style
   lengthwise into 1″
   pieces
2 tablespoons olive or
   peanut oil
Coarse salt and red
   crushed pepper, as de-
   sired

Vitamins A, B and C—especially A for eyes, and the minerals are fine for the development of bones, cartilage tissue, tendons and teeth.

Sauté the seasoned green beans in butter or oil or water over low heat. Stir constantly until warm. (2 to 4 minutes)

VEGETABLES

For variation: GREEN BEANS ALMONDINE

Almonds are a source of natural concentrated vitamins.

Add thinly slivered almonds, raw and salted somewhat.

GREEN BEANS AND CORN

2 cups green beans
1½ cups raw corn cut off cob
1 teaspoon grated onion
Coarse salt and coarse black pepper, as desired
1 cup certified raw milk
3 tablespoons whole wheat flour
Coarse salt and pepper, as desired

A combination that coordinates into a perfect bone and muscle tissue builder full of vitamins and minerals.

Sauté green beans, corn, seasonings and onion in butter or oil over slow heat stirring over and over until warm. Creaming: Warm the milk and whole wheat flour with oil and seasoning over low heat until thick. For Au Gratin, add 3 tablespoons grated Parmesan cheese or ½ cup diced Provoloni cheese.

68

GREEN BEANS WITH BACON

2 cups green beans, cut
  French style
4 strips Canadian bacon *Fast tissue and bone builder.*
2 tablespoons olive oil
2 tablespoons grated
  Parmesan cheese
Coarse salt and red
  crushed pepper, as de-
  sired

Sauté the beans, bacon, onion and seasonings in oil, over low heat stirring constantly until warm. (2-4 min.) Yellow string beans may be used in the same way. For variation and color use both together in the same recipe.

BUTTERED HOMINY

2 cups hominy grits
  soaked in water with 4
  tablespoons coarse salt   *High mineral content and added*
  for 24 hours   *protein make this cereal food a*
4 tablespoons butter or   *good balanced carbohydrate for*
  to taste   *energy and body building.*
Coarse salt and red
  crushed pepper, as de-
  sired

69

Drain water from hominy. Saute with seasonings and butter over very slow heat. Stir constantly until warm. (2-4 minutes) Hominy Au Gratin: Add grated Parmesan cheese, as desired.

SAUTÉED KALE

1 bunch fresh Kale
2 tablespoons butter,
   olive, or peanut oil
Coarse salt and coarse
   black pepper, as de-
   sired

Lots of Vitamin A and calcium —good for the eyes, and bone, teeth and muscle building.

Cut the kale into 1" pieces. Sauté with seasonings in oil or butter over very low heat stirring constantly until warm. (4 minutes) Kohlrabi, and Leeks may be sautéed in the same way.

LEEKS AND WHOLE WHEAT SAUTÉ

1 bunch leeks
4 tablespoons whole
   wheat flour
3 tablespoons butter or
   olive oil

A natural sweet for body.

Coarse salt and coarse
   black pepper, as de-
   sired

Cut leeks into small pieces. Toss with flour and sauté with seasonings in butter or oil, stirring frequently until warm. (2-4 minutes)

GREEN BABY LIMA BEANS

2 cups baby lima beans
3 tablespoons butter or
   olive oil
Coarse salt and red
   crushed pepper, as de-
   sired

Fresh source of Vitamins A, B, C, and minerals for body energy and building.

Sauté limas with seasonings and butter, oil or water over low heat until warm. Stir frequently.

BEAN-CORN-TASH

1 cup fresh lima beans
1 cup raw corn, cut off
   cob
3 tablespoons butter,
   olive, peanut oil or
   water

Highly nutritious, especially the peppers.

Coarse salt and red
    crushed pepper, as
    desired
½ diced green pepper
½ minced onion

Combine beans, corn, green pepper and onion with butter, oil or water and seasonings. Stir over low heat, constantly until warm. (2-4 minutes)

LIMA BEANS AND TOMATOES

Use
3 fresh tomatoes instead
    of 1 cup raw corn
    in recipe above for
    Bean-Corn-Tash
Use all other ingredients
    plus ⅛ teaspoon ore-
    gano

Extremely wholesome. Tomatoes increase alkalinity in the blood and remove toxins, especially uric acid.

Follow the same directions as in Bean-Corn-Tash.

SAUTÉED LENTILS

2 cups dried lentils,
    soaked for 48 hours in
    water and 4 table-
    spoons coarse salt.
    Change water 4 times.

A staple food. Beneficial in body building. Use just enough water to cover and be absorbed by the

1 teaspoon grated onion
4 tablespoons olive or
   peanut oil
Coarse salt and red
   crushed pepper,
   as desired

food, to prevent mineral loss in the soaking.

Sauté the lentils slowly with onion and seasonings in oil or butter. Stir frequently until warm.

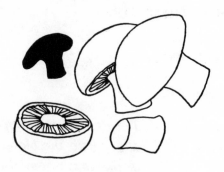

MUSHROOMS AND VEGETABLES

2 cups diced
   mushrooms
½ cup fresh raw certi-
   fied cream
1 large minced onion
½ cup celery leaves,
   cut up
½ green pepper, diced
1 tablespoon olive oil
   or butter

The Fe salts in mushrooms make this food important for blood building.

☞

VEGETABLES

Coarse salt and red
    crushed pepper,
    as desired
1 egg (optional)

Sear the onion in oil and seasonings quickly over a high heat. Add cream over slow heat, stirring constantly until warm. If egg is added, add to the whole mixture away from the heat and at the very end of the process of preparing. Add mushrooms last.

BUTTERED MUSHROOMS

1 lb. fresh mushrooms,
    diced
4 tablespoons butter
Coarse salt and coarse
    black pepper, as de-
    sired

The Fe salts and copper indicated above help the blood. No longer is the mushroom used only for exotic flavor and decor.

Sauté the mushrooms in butter, stirring over low heat until warm.

MUSHROOMS AND WILD RICE

2 cups wild rice, soaked
    overnight
2 cups diced fresh
    mushrooms
1 green pepper, diced

Much iron, calcium, and phosphorous as well as ash in wild rice. Since unbleached and with

74

1 diced onion
2 stalks celery
  with leaves
3 tablespoons olive or
  peanut oil
Coarse salt and red
  crushed pepper,
  as desired

cellulose covers it is perfect to pre-vent nervous disorders, and heart trouble. With mushrooms and mineral salts good for anemia, and diarrhea.

Drain rice if any water is left. Combine with oil and sea-sonings. In another pan, sear quickly over very high heat, all vegetables except mushrooms, turning constantly. When these are hot (2 minutes) remove from heat, stir in mushrooms, cover pan and let set for about 1 minute. Warm the rice in the vegetables after heating for one minute in another pan. Combine all ingredients and add some soya sauce before serving to give it an oriental flavor.

ONIONS

8 small white onions
4 tablespoons olive, corn
  or peanut oil
Coarse salt and red
  crushed pepper,
  as desired

Vitamin A content to aid in the care of eyes and eye membranes and the prevention of night blind-ness. Full of phosphorous.

Peel and wash onions. Sauté in oil or butter or just water. Use low heat, stir constantly until warm. (2-4 minutes)

75

SCALDED ONIONS

Use same ingredients as
above, plus 2 cups
water

*Less gaseous in this state than in
the raw.*

Heat water. Place onions and seasonings in water; let
stand 4 minutes.

ONIONS AU GRATIN

Add to the above ingre-
dients:
  2 tablespoons whole
    wheat flour
  6 tablespoons grated
    Parmesan cheese
  dash oregano
  Coarse salt and coarse
    black pepper, as de-
    sired

*The added protein in cheese and
vitamins in wheat flour make for
quite a complete vegetable food.*

Mix onion in flour, cheese and seasonings. Sauté quickly
over high flame turning constantly until warm. (3 minutes)

CREAMED ONIONS

4 sliced onions, or 8
  small whole onions
1 cup raw certified milk
3 tablespoons whole
  wheat flour
2 tablespoons butter or
  olive oil
Coarse salt and red
  crushed pepper

Rich in blood and tissue building elements, with minerals and Vitamins A, B and C. Milk adds to the protein value in the recipe.

Warm the milk, and stir in the flour, the oil or butter and seasonings. Add the onions and stir constantly until warm. (3 minutes)

TOMATO AND ONION SAUTE

4 onions, sliced or whole
4 tomatoes, cut into
  pieces
1 diced celery stalk
Dash oregano
Basil leaf
3 tablespoons olive oil
1 raw egg
Coarse salt and red
  crushed pepper,
  as desired

Higher Vitamin C value with the addition of tomatoes. Tasty as well as perfect combination for young and old, for increased vim and vigor.

VEGETABLES

Sauté all the vegetables and seasonings with oil over slow heat, stirring constantly until warm. (2-4 minutes) Beat egg and stir into warm vegetables which have been turned into a bowl from which it will be served.

OKRA

3 cups okra, sliced into
  1″ pieces
4 tablespoons olive, corn
  or peanut oil
Dash oregano
Coarse salt and coarse
  black pepper, as de-
  sired

High in Vitamin A (good for the eyes), medium in B (energy and body building), and more in C (good for strengthening the small blood vessels and gums).

Slice okra thin. Saute over fast flame stirring constantly until warm with the oil and seasonings. (2-3 minutes)

PARSNIPS SAUTÉ

4-6 parsnips
  4 tablespoons olive,
    peanut oil or butter
Coarse salt and red
  crushed pepper,
  as desired

High in minerals, especially calcium and phosphorous which are needed for bones and teeth.

Roll parsnips in oil and seasonings and then sauté over a slow flame stirring constantly until warm. (3-5 minutes)

78

SCALDED PARSNIPS

Add 2 cups water to the
  ingredients above

A variation of the root, as valuable as the recipe above.

Heat water. Place parsnips and seasoning in water; let stand. (4 minutes) Remove from water. Add oil or butter, and seasonings to serve.

PARSNIP CASSEROLE

2 cups diced raw parsnips
1 diced onion
1 diced green pepper
1 stalk celery, cut up
3 tablespoons whole wheat flour
1 beaten raw egg
3 tablespoons olive or peanut oil
4 tomatoes, if desired
Coarse salt and red crushed pepper, as desired

An example of a mixture of ingredients that enhance each other and make a perfect wholesome dish.

Combine all vegetables, except tomatoes, with flour and sear over a high flame. (2-3 minutes) Add the mashed tomatoes. When warm, place in casserole, fold in the beaten egg and serve.

VEGETABLES

PARSNIPS AND CARROTS

1½ cups diced parsnips
1½ cups diced carrots
1 stalk celery, cut up
1 tablespoon grated onion or garlic clove
1 diced green pepper
1 raw egg
Coarse salt and red crushed pepper, as desired

Both roots beneficial in blood and tissue development, especially for eyes, hair, skin and mucous membranes. The duet is pretty to look at, tasty to eat and full of energy value for the body.

Combine all vegetables with seasonings and sear in oil quickly over fast heat until warm. Beat up egg and add to the mixture which has been placed in a covered casserole.

GREEN PEAS AND CREAMED PEAS

2 cups fresh or frozen green peas
3 tablespoons butter, olive or peanut oil
1 teaspoon grated onion, or scallion
Coarse salt and red crushed pepper, as desired

Rich in vitamins and minerals and beneficial as well as economical to the body if eaten raw or slightly warmed.

80

Chop scallions and sear first. Add peas and sauté over slow heat stirring constantly until warm. (2 minutes) Add the salt and pepper just before serving.

Creamed:
  2 tablespoons whole
      wheat flour   *More protein.*
  ½ cup certified raw milk

Make the whole wheat flour into a paste with water and add to the warm milk, butter and seasonings. Warm slowly and stir constantly and then add the peas.

For variation:

Add 1 cup diced smoked ham or 3 slices of raw bacon, cut into small pieces.

PEAS AND CARROTS

1½ cups raw green peas
  1 cup raw sliced
      carrots   *Carotene in carrots so important*
  1 clove of garlic or 1 *for the eyes.*
      scallion
  3 tablespoons butter
      or olive oil
Coarse salt and red
      crushed pepper,
      as desired

81

VEGETABLES

Sauté over slow flame stirring constantly until warm and serve. (2 minutes) For variation, one may add chopped scallions.

CREAMED PEAS AND CORN

Add to the above ingre-
dients:
   2 tablespoons whole
      wheat flour
   ½ cup certified raw
      milk
   1 cup fresh corn
      kernels (cut off
      cob)

Rich and economical protein of utmost benefit to the body if eaten raw or slightly warmed.

Make the whole wheat flour into a paste with water and add the milk, butter or oil and seasonings. Warm mildly and add the peas and onion. Use a slow flame to warm thoroughly. (2-3 minutes)

PEAS AND CARROTS AND CORN

1½ cups raw green peas
   1 cup sliced raw
      carrots
   3 tablespoons olive oil
      or butter

Your ABCs, and mineral value to boot.

82

Coarse salt, sea salt and
     pepper
  1 cup raw fresh corn
     kernels (cut off
     cob)

Sauté over a slow flame the peas, carrots, corn, scallion or garlic if desired, and seasoning. Stir constantly until warm. (2-3 minutes)

PEAS AND ASPARAGUS

1½ cups fresh or frozen
     green peas
  1 cup raw asparagus,
     diced into ½ inch
     pieces
  2 teaspoons onion, or
     scallion chopped
  3 tablespoons olive,
     corn or peanut oil
Coarse salt and red
     crushed pepper,
     as desired

Bones and teeth fare well here. Very nourishing. Usually a favorite, especially with pregnant women.

Sauté all ingredients over low flame, stirring constantly until warm. (2-3 minutes)

PEAS AU GRATIN

2 cups fresh green peas
½ cup grated Parmesan
cheese
½ cup raw certified
milk
4 tablespoons wheat
flour
3 tablespoons butter or
oil (olive, corn or
peanut)
Coarse salt and red
crushed pepper,
as desired

High in protein. The cheese and milk contribute to body building, repair and energy.

Warm milk and add whole wheat flour, butter or oil, cheese and seasonings. Blend in peas. (2-3 minutes)

PEAS POTENTE

2 cups fresh green peas
2 cups corn flour
1 scallion, chopped
1 tablespoon Romano
cheese
1 cup diced fresh mush-
rooms
1 tablespoon olive, corn
or peanut oil
5 cups water, less if
thickness is desired

A tasteful rich tissue builder, a real gourmet taste that is basic in Vitamins A, B and C and mineral value.

Coarse salt and red
  crushed pepper,
  as desired

Warm water with flour, stirring constantly. Add peas,
scallion (pre-seared in frying pan with oil or butter),
cheese and seasonings. Stir constantly over low flame until
warm. Remove and add mushrooms. Let stand a minute
and serve.

SAUTÉED PEPPERS

3 sliced peppers, seeds
  retained
1 scallion, cut up
3 tablespoons olive,
  corn or peanut
  oil, or water
Coarse salt and red
  crushed pepper,
  as desired

*These vitamin packed A, B, C's
are nutrients for body and blood.
High in nutritional value. The
seeds have protein properties and
serve as true vitamins.*

Sauté the peppers and onion with oil and seasonings. Use
a high flame and turn constantly until warm. (2 minutes)

BROILED PEPPERS

4 large green peppers
Olive oil

Lemon peel, grated
Lemon juice, to taste
Coarse salt

High nutritional value. The seeds have protein properties.

Broil peppers over high flame. Retain peel or remove as desired. Cut into long strips and combine with oil, salt, lemon juice and lemon rind. Serve as a vegetable or as a relish.

GREEN PEPPER AND TOMATO SAUCE

2 sliced green peppers,
   with seeds
4 diced large tomatoes
2 thinly sliced scallions
1 beaten raw egg
Dash oregano
Basil leaf
Coarse salt and red
   crushed pepper,
   as desired
3 tablespoons olive,
   corn or peanut oil

Again the addition of Vitamin C in tomatoes contributes towards keeping small blood vessels strong and well formed; aids in care of gums, prevents bleeding there, and helps to heal wounds.

Sear the green pepper and scallions over a very fast flame. Season the tomatoes and stir into the peppers and scallions over a low flame until all are warm. Turn into a heated serving dish and fold in the beaten egg very quickly to prevent curdling of the egg. The beaten egg then serves as a sauce.

STUFFED GREEN PEPPERS

4 green peppers
2 cups Italian Avorio
  Rice soaked 4 hours
1 onion, finely chopped
1 celery stalk, finely
  chopped with leaves
1 cup fresh mushrooms,
  diced
3 tablespoons olive,
  corn or peanut oil
Coarse salt and red
  crushed pepper,
  as desired

A pleasant variation and one usually well liked. The combination of ingredients make for a cache of all the Vitamins A, B, and C plus minerals. The rice is high in thiamine.

Scoop out the insides of the peppers. Sear the peppers quickly under a flame or in a broiler. In a separate pan sear over a fast flame the insides of the peppers, the onion, and celery. Turn the flame low, add the rice and stir until warm. Remove from heat and add the raw mushrooms to the mixture. Then stuff the combination into the seared pepper shells and place in oven at 150 to 200° for 5 minutes. Leave in oven for another five or ten minutes. The peppers will be slightly wilted, but will have retained vital values.

RAW POTATO STEAKS

2 large well scrubbed,
   but *not* peeled pota-
   toes (Idaho type)
2 tablespoons olive or
   peanut oil
Coarse salt and red
   crushed pepper,
   as desired
Dash oregano
1 clove garlic, minced

Close in taste to the Chinese water chestnut. Full of Vitamins A, B and C and minerals. A highly nourishing, very economical tissue builder.

Cover bottom of frying pan with film of oil. Get the pan very hot. Place the seasoned potato slices (⅛ inch thickness) in pan and sear rapidly until they are just slightly tan on each side. Cover with top of pan and allow to stand for about a minute. They will be half raw and hot and very tasty.

RAW COTTAGE FRIES

2 large potatoes in
   jackets
2 tablespoons olive or
   peanut oil
½ onion grated or garlic
   clove
Oregano
Coarse salt and red
   crushed pepper,
   as desired

The potato with skin is full of vitamins and minerals.

88

Scrub and slice potatoes ¼ inch thick and place in pan with oil. Season the potatoes. Use high flame and stir as soon as potatoes are bronzed on one side. Cover and remove from heat. Let stand for about a minute and then serve in a covered casserole. They will be crunchy and delicious.

POTATO PANCAKES

2 cups grated raw
   potato
1 egg   *Easily digested this way. In the*
½ grated onion, or scal- *skins are the vitamins and min-*
   lion, chopped   *erals.*
Peanut or olive oil
Coarse salt and red
   crushed pepper,
   as desired

Mix the potatoes, onion and egg together with the seasonings. Cover the bottom of the pan with a film of oil, drop in spoonfuls of the mixture in the form of pancakes and warm over very low flame until they can be turned over. Remove to a warm platter as soon as the pancakes hold together. They will be hot and tasty. (1 minute for each pancake)

For variation:

Add grated Parmesan cheese, chopped ham or bacon.

VEGETABLES

"FRENCH FRIES"

3 potatoes in jackets, cut
in strips lengthwise, 1"
thick
2 tablespoons peanut or
olive oil
Coarse salt and red
crushed peppers,
as desired

The perennial favorite of the American, especially the teen-age set! All of the elements mentioned in recipes with potatoes are here. However with a few more calories. Good for body heat. Fine for a quick pick-up in energy.

Season and fry rapidly in shallow oil until slightly tanned not browned. These will be half raw but very tasty. They resemble the Chinese water chestnut this way, or have a more nutty flavor.

RAW POTATO, ITALIAN STYLE

3 potatoes, sliced fine
1 grated onion
1 large green pepper,
sliced with seeds
1 teaspoon olive oil
1 raw egg for each serv-
ing
Coarse salt and red
crushed pepper,
as desired

Another variation of potato, with all of the vitamins and minerals mentioned in potato recipes. The egg adds the protein touch that balances the nutrient value.

Season and use the oil as a film on a pan and sear the potatoes, pepper and onion. When bronzed, turn over like an omelet, bronze the other side, remove from flame and place in individual pottery covered casserole dishes. Warm the eggs in their shells for about a minute, and break over each serving, covering at once.

"BAKED POTATOES" (AIR-DRIED)

Wash potatoes, heat oven and then turn down to about 150-200°. Put the potatoes in for about five minutes with heat on. Then leave them in oven with heat turned off for about 30 minutes. Wrap potatoes in a damp cloth or aluminum foil and let remain another 10 minutes. These will be half baked and will be moist instead of dry and mealy. If one has a rotisserie one can spear the potatoes on a skewer and let rotate around for about five minutes, and they will be baked sufficiently to be eaten and enjoyed. Also, one can put them into hot coals in an outdoor barbecue or an inside habache.

SCALLOPED POTATOES

3 small thinly sliced potatoes, in jackets
1 small onion, grated
½ cup raw certified milk

Calcium, phosphorous and iron are just what the body needs for vim, vigor and growth.

☞

91

2 tablespoons whole
  wheat flour
3 or 4 tablespoons
  Parmesan cheese
  or Cheddar
1 tablespoon olive oil
  or butter
Coarse salt and red
  crushed pepper,
  as desired

Using the oil as a film on pan, sear over high heat the seasoned potato slices and onion. Turn over as soon as bronzed and add milk, flour (mixed), cheese and stir constantly until warm. Be sure not to overheat the milk. Place in oven for about 10 minutes at 150 to 200°. Serve with another sprinkling of cheese.

GERMAN STYLE POTATOES

2 medium sized pota-
  toes with skins
1 tablespoon grated
  onion
1 cup kernels of raw
  corn, cut off cob
1 tablespoon finely
  chopped chives
1 tablespoon finely
  chopped parsley
½ cup finely chopped

A European flavor here, but the same properties of the valuable potato, plus the high nutrient values in the other vegetables.

green pepper
2 tablespoons olive,
    corn or peanut oil
Coarse salt and coarse
    black pepper, as de-
    sired

Cut the potatoes into 1" width slices. Sear in pan on film of oil. The slices will be hard inside but hot . . . Dice these, cover and leave in pan (set aside from the heat). In another pan, sear the onion and pepper, then combine with the corn, parsley and diced potato. Stir occasionally over a low heat until warm. (3-4 minutes)

POTATO CHOP SUEY

2 medium sized potatoes
    in jackets
1 onion, or scallion, cut
    fine
1 chopped green pepper
    with seeds
2 stalks celery, chopped
    with leaves
2 raw eggs
Dash oregano
2 tablespoons olive,
    corn or peanut oil
Coarse salt and coarse
    black pepper, as de-
    sired

The final Chinese touch with the varied vegetables. The end result is a full-fledged well of vitamins and minerals.

Cut the potatoes into 1" slices. Sear in pan on film of oil. The slices will be raw inside, but hot. Dice these, cover and leave in pan and set aside from the heat. In another pan sear the onion, pepper and celery with seasoning desired. Be sure that these vegetables are only heated, not cooked. Mix the vegetables with the potatoes in a serving bowl and stir in the beaten eggs which serve as a sauce. *Soya bean sauce* may be used for flavoring (a real addition to the Chinese touch).

PUMPKIN GRATED

2 cups grated raw pumpkin
3 or 4 tablespoons butter
1 teaspoon honey
Coarse salt and coarse black pepper, as desired

Surprisingly high in Vitamin A. Full of carotene for the care of the eyes. The seeds when dried out, are another source of pure protein and one of the most perfect of nature's own vitamins.

Mix the raw pumpkin with seasonings and melted butter and warm in pan over very slow heat stirring constantly. (3 minutes)

DICED PUMPKIN

2 cups diced raw
  pumpkin
2 tablespoons butter
2 tablespoons honey
Coarse salt and coarse
  black pepper, as de-
  sired

Same as for Pumpkin Grated.

Combine the pumpkin with butter and seasonings. Using a low flame, stir this mixture constantly until warm. (2-3 minutes)

CREAMED RUTABAGAS

2 cups diced rutabagas
3 tablespoons butter or
  olive oil
1 teaspoon honey
1 cup certified raw milk
Coarse salt and coarse
  black pepper, as de-
  sired

Another unusual vegetable that is full of Vitamins A, B and C and minerals—all ready to aid the body in bones, teeth, nerve tissue and heart.

Sauté rutabagas with butter and seasonings over slow flame turning constantly until warm. In separate pan, warm milk with butter and flour (mixed with water). Stir in the sautéed rutabagas and serve.

This may be varied as "Au Gratin" with the addition of ½ cup of grated Parmesan cheese.

95

SEARED SALSIFY

2 raw salsify, diced (oyster plant)
3 tablespoons olive or peanut oil
3 tablespoons whole wheat flour
Coarse salt and coarse black pepper, as desired

A root, rich in elements that build blood and muscle tissue. Rarely used here in America, but can be fixed in delicious manner for a real change. A poor man's version of oysters.

Sprinkle salsify with flour and seasonings. Sear in oil rapidly over high heat, turning constantly. Cover pan for about 3 minutes and serve with melted butter.

SWEET POTATO STEAKS

2 sweet potatoes in jackets, sliced 1" thick
1-2 tablespoons olive, corn or peanut oil
3 tablespoons honey
Coarse salt and coarse black pepper, as desired

The festive sweet potato has a rich supply of Vitamin A as well as B and C and minerals. The carotene aids the eyes. Fine vegetable starch for energy. The natural sugar is excellent for body vigor.

Place seasoned potatoes in pan with film of oil. Sear rapidly over very high heat until the potatoes are bronzed on both sides. If desired, pour honey over them, just before serving.

HONEYED SWEET POTATOES

Same ingredients as
    above
Slice the potatoes, thin

The natural sugar here and the honey increase the value for body energy and vigor. Perfect change and a real holiday treat.

Same as above. After pouring the honey over potatoes, let stand five minutes before serving.

SWEET POTATO PANCAKES

2 cups raw sweet pota-
    toes, grated
1 or 2 beaten eggs
1 tablespoon honey
3 tablespoons whole
    wheat flour
2 tablespoons olive, corn
    or peanut oil
Coarse salt and coarse
    black pepper, as de-
    sired

Another variation of the elements in sweet potatoes.

VEGETABLES

Combine the potato and all the other ingredients and drop in spoonfuls on film of oil in pan. Warm like a pancake over very low heat until it can be turned over.

SWEET POTATO STICKS

2 sweet potatoes, cut in
  strips 1″ thick
2 tablespoons peanut oil   *Do not cook the fragile Vitamin*
Coarse salt and coarse   *C out of the potato!*
  black pepper, as de-
  sired

Sear the potatoes on film of oil very quickly until slightly tanned, not browned. These will be half raw, but hot and tasty.

SPINACH

1 lb. fresh spinach
1 clove garlic, cut
3 tablespoons olive oil,   *Rich in Vitamin B-12, it builds*
  or butter   *the hemoglobin in the blood.*
Coarse salt and red
  crushed pepper, if
  desired

Wash spinach thoroughly in cold water several times. Cut off roots and then tear spinach into small pieces. Place spinach into saucepan, combine with oil, salt, and garlic and stir constantly until *warm*. (2 minutes)

98

CREAMED SPINACH

Same ingredients as
above with additions:
  ½ cup certified raw
    milk
  3 tablespoons whole
    wheat flour
  1 tablespoon olive
    oil
Coarse salt and red
    crushed pepper, if
    desired

The low calorie value of spinach permits creaming with peace of mind. In addition to the values stated above, the raw milk helps to complete the protein value; the whole wheat is carbohydrate for food energy. Vitamin B with its riboflavin niacin and thiamine, is excellent for nerves under "stress."

Prepare spinach as described above for recipe SPINACH. In another saucepan, warm milk slightly, add flour (mixed with some water) and butter until hot. Combine this with spinach.

SPINACH SPECIAL

1 lb. spinach
2 tablespoons olive oil
  or butter
1 tablespoon grated on-
  ion
2 eggs, beaten
Coarse salt and red
  crushed pepper

Calorie low, and full of minerals especially iron.

Wash spinach carefully, place in saucepan with oil or butter and onion, and season to taste. Stir constantly over low heat until the spinach is warm. (1 to 2 minutes) Combine with the whipped eggs, serve.

CREAMED SPINACH AU GRATIN

Note ingredients in
  CREAMED SPIN-
  ACH
Add:
  ¼ cup grated Parmesan or Cheddar cheese

Even more nourishing with the cheese. A riot of nutrients with Vitamins A, B, and C and minerals for the body.

Follow directions for CREAMED SPINACH. Add the cheese along with milk.

SPINACH VINAIGRA

1 lb. fresh spinach
3 tablespoons wine or cider vinegar
2 tablespoons honey
Coarse salt and red crushed pepper if desired

The stimulation of the vinegar and honey add zest to the spinach.

Wash spinach, tear, place in saucepan, season and warm over a fast flame, turning constantly. Blend wine vinegar and honey together, and add to the spinach. Cover

100

saucepan and remove from heat until ready to serve. (2 minutes)

SPINACH CAKES

2 cups fresh spinach, chopped fine
2 eggs, beaten
1 tablespoon grated onion
3 tablespoons whole wheat flour
2 tablespoons olive, corn or peanut oil
½ teaspoon coarse salt
¼ teaspoon red crushed pepper

A real surprise in pancakes. Full of the benefits of spinach, mentioned in the above recipes.

Combine spinach with eggs, onion, flour, and oil seasonings. Drop cakes on pan with light film of oil and using low heat, turn them over as soon as they have the consistency necessary. (½ minute on each side)

BABY YELLOW SQUASH

2 cups yellow squash, sliced ½" thick
3 tablespoons oil (olive, corn or peanut) or butter

Carotene plus in squash.

½ teaspoon coarse salt
¼ teaspoon coarse
black pepper

Combine squash with oil or butter or water and season to taste. Stir constantly over high heat until squash is warm. (2 minutes)

MASHED YELLOW SQUASH

2 cups yellow squash
3 tablespoons olive oil,
or butter
½ teaspoon coarse salt
¼ teaspoon coarse
black pepper

The easily digested carotene plus vegetable protein. Good for the infant and the aged because it is so easily chewed.

Combine squash with oil or butter and seasoning in saucepan. Stir constantly. Put into electric blender and make smooth. Heat over low flame until warmed. (2-3 minutes)

HONEYED SQUASH

2 cups diced summer
squash
4 tablespoons honey
2 tablespoons butter
Coarse salt and coarse
black pepper if de-
sired

The natural sugar makes this a festive dish abounding in energy for the body.

102

In a saucepan combine squash, honey, butter and seasonings; stir constantly over a low heat until warm. (2-3 minutes)

SQUASH AND TOMATOES

1 cup sliced squash, yellow or green (Italian zucchini)
1 cup mashed fresh tomatoes
1 tablespoon grated onion, or 1 scallion
2 tablespoons olive oil
Dash oregano
Coarse salt and red crushed pepper

The added Vitamin C in tomato stimulates the vigor of the food for the care of small blood vessels and gums.

In a saucepan combine squash, tomatoes, onion, oil and seasonings. Stir constantly over a low heat until warm. (2-3 minutes)

TOMATOES

3 fresh tomatoes
1 tablespoon grated onion, or 1 scallion
1 tablespoon honey
⅛ teaspoon oregano

Vitamin C!

☞

⅛ teaspoon basil leaf,
   crushed
Coarse salt and red
   crushed pepper

Combine the tomatoes, onion, honey and seasoning, if desired. Over high heat, stir constantly until warm. (2-3 minutes)

BROILED TOMATOES

Same ingredients as
   above.

Cut tomatoes in halves, broil under high heat (1 minute on each side) and then season and serve.

TOMATOES AU GRATIN

Same ingredients as for
   TOMATOES Add to
   this:
   4 tablespoons grated
      cheese, Parmesan,
      Cheddar, or
      Provolone
   2 tablespoons whole
      wheat flour
   1 tablespoon olive oil

Cheese adds to the tissue building properties of the recipe.

104

Coarse salt and red
   crushed pepper,
   fresh pepper, if
   possible.

Combine all ingredients, and add cheese, flour and seasonings. Heat until hot and serve.

ESCALLOPED TOMATOES

3 tomatoes
1 grated small onion or
   1 scallion
1 diced fresh green
   pepper
2 stalks celery, chopped
2 tablespoons olive, corn
   or peanut oil
3 tablespoons whole
   wheat flour
3 tablespoons cornmeal
Dash oregano
1 Basil leaf
½ teaspoon coarse salt
   and fresh red pepper

High Vitamin B of whole wheat flour and minerals aid in body building, energy, bone and teeth contruction and repair.

Sear onion, pepper and celery over high heat. Combine with tomatoes and oil with seasonings, flour and cornmeal. Warm over a low heat and serve. Grated cheese may be added.

TOMATO-CORN SURPRISE

4 tomatoes, quartered
1 cup corn, cut off cob
2 scallions, cut
½ green pepper,
    chopped
Olive oil
½ teaspoon coarse salt
¼ teaspoon red crushed
    pepper, or fresh red
    pepper

Contains cellulose, good for elimination. The incompleteness of protein in corn is overcome by the tomato.

Add tomatoes and corn to the already seared onion and peppers. Add the seasonings and warm over a low heat. (2 minutes)

YELLOW TURNIP STRIPS

6-8 fresh yellow turnips,
      sliced lengthwise
  2 tablespoons butter,
      olive, or peanut oil
 ½ teaspoon coarse salt
 ¼ teaspoon coarse
      black pepper

Vitamins B and C and minerals, especially calcium and phosphorus, all lead to energy. Also aids in blood building, and bone, teeth, and nerve tissue structure and repair. Carotene is for eyes and eye membranes.

Sauté the strips of turnips on film of oil or butter. Turn over once, season and serve. Use a high heat when searing. (2 minutes)

MASHED YELLOW TURNIPS

Same ingredients as
 above

Blend in an electric mixer. Heat and serve.

WHITE TURNIPS

2 cups diced turnips
2 tablespoons olive, corn
 or peanut oil
1 tablespoon grated
 onion
½ teaspoon coarse salt
¼ teaspoon coarse
 black pepper

Like all root vegetables, a good source of minerals.

Place ingredients into saucepan, stir constantly and warm over low heat. This also may be mashed in an electric mixer. Add butter or oil and season. (2-3 minutes)

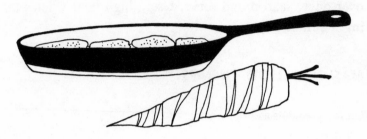

TURNIP PANCAKES

2 cups grated turnips
2 eggs, beaten
1 grated small onion
3 tablespoons whole
   wheat flour
1 teaspoon honey
1 tablespoon olive, corn
   or peanut oil
Coarse salt and coarse
   black pepper, as
   desired

A pleasant variation of the vegetable for the replenishment of vitamins, minerals and protein.

Combine all the ingredients. Use an electric blender, if you wish. Drop as patties on a film of oil in pan. Use low heat. As soon as patties take form, turn them over. (1 minute on each side) Do not brown!

TURNIP GREENS

1 lb. turnip greens
2 tablespoons olive or
   peanut oil
2 cloves of garlic,
   minced
Coarse salt and coarse
   black pepper, as de-
   sired

Chlorophyll to sweeten the mouth.

Chop the greens into small pieces. Put into saucepan with oil, garlic and seasoning. Add ½ cup of water if necessary. Usually the water on the leaves is enough. Stir constantly over low heat until warm. Cover pot until warm (away from heat). (1 minute)

TURNIP GREEN PATTIES

Same ingredients as
   above
Add:
   2 eggs, beaten
   3 tablespoons whole
      wheat flour

Good for skin, and excellent for elimination.

Combine all ingredients and drop into pan on film of oil. Use low heat. When formed as pancake, turn over. (½ minute on each side)

TURNIP GREEN PATTIES AND HAM

Same ingredients as for
  TURNIP GREEN
  PATTIES   *Added animal protein and fat en-*
Add: *rich this dish.*
  1 cup cubed raw
     smoked ham

Combine ingredients and proceed as usual with pancakes.
(as above) *Do not brown.* (½ minute on each side)

4. SALADS

TOSSED SALAD

1 head crisp iceberg
   lettuce
6 leaves romaine lettuce
1 cucumber
3 ripe tomatoes
1 mild Italian or Ber-
   muda onion

The combined ingredients have a higher nutritional value than when they are eaten separately. Greater energy is released as they supplement one another.

Chop up or tear lettuce, cube the cucumber and onion, quarter the tomatoes leaving one for garnish. Sliced green pepper may also be used for taste and garnish.

SALADS

For salad dressing:

1 cup raw certified milk
or cream
1 raw egg
1 teaspoon lemon juice
1 teaspoon honey
1 teaspoon dry mustard
Coarse salt and black
pepper
3 tablespoons olive oil,
or corn oil

Whip up together thoroughly or use electric mixer.

MULTI-COLORED FRESH VEGETABLE SALAD

1 cucumber
1 red onion
2 crisp carrots
2 stalks celery, with
leaves
8 red radishes
1 head crisp lettuce
1 green pepper, diced

Complete vitalizing combination. Carotene high—good for eyes, skin, and hair.

Chop and cut up all vegetables. Chill and serve with olive, corn or peanut oil plus wine vinegar, or lemon and seasonings.

SUMMER SALAD

1 bunch of scallions
  (4-5)
1 bunch of watercress
1 bunch of radishes
1 large cucumber

A mineral salad this! Phosphorus for more building and repair. Watercress, with its high vitamin content, is perfect for clear skin and bright eyes.

Cut up scallions, dice up cucumber, and cut radishes in roselike shape. Arrange on thoroughly washed watercress. Serve with dressing of olive, corn or peanut oil, wine vinegar, or lemon juice. Salt and pepper to taste.

SALAD A LA OLIVES AND CHEESE

1 bunch watercress
¼ cup diced cheese
  (any aged cheese,
  like Cheddar)
12 large green olives
Olive oil and lemon
  juice in equal parts

Olives are not for decoration here; they are a source of calcium for the needed Vitamin D.

Wash watercress and break up into small pieces. Cut up olives and blend with cheese and add to watercress. Toss with a dressing of olive oil and lemon juice, or wine vinegar.

113

TOMATO AND CORN SALAD

4-6 ripe tomatoes
  2 ears of corn, raw
  1 basil leaf
  2 tablespoons olive oil
Dash oregano and Italian dried herbs
  1 large red onion or scallion
Coarse salt and red crushed pepper, as desired

Very tasty blend, vital in Vitamins A, B and C. Corn kernels are a good source of B.

Cut tomatoes into quarters. Wash ears of corn and cut kernels off cobs. Slice onion thin and blend with tomatoes and corn. Mix in olive oil, salt, and red crushed pepper.

POTATO SALAD

4 medium-sized potatoes
4 ripe tomatoes
1 large red onion
1 large green pepper
Basil leaves
Dash oregano
Coarse salt and red crushed pepper, as desired

Potatoes here taste like Chinese chestnuts used in chop suey. Plenty of vitamin C in potato skins. Beneficial for teeth.

114

Dice the raw potatoes, cut up tomatoes, onion, and green pepper. Blend with one or two tablespoonfuls of olive or peanut oil, coarse salt and pepper, and other seasonings.

LETTUCE SALAD

½ head iceberg lettuce
½ head romaine lettuce
¼ head escarole
¼ head chicory
2 tablespoons olive oil
½ teaspoon coarse salt
¼ teaspoon coarse
    black pepper, if
    desired

High in Vitamin A and low in calories. Vitamin E good for muscles, may prevent paralysis, and research may prove lack of Vitamin E a cause of sterility.

Cut up or tear up into pieces. Blend with olive oil. Add salt and pepper. Serve crisp and chilled.

SHREDDED CARROT AND RAW BEET SALAD

1 bunch fresh carrots
3 raw red beets
1 head of lettuce
2 tablespoons olive oil
1 tablespoon lemon
    juice
Coarse salt and pepper

A vegetable bank of Vitamin A, so good for the membranes of the eyes, good healthy skin, and bone growth. Natural sugar for energy. Good natural laxative.

115

SALADS

Grate or shred carrots and beets. Arrange in separate groups on lettuce leaves. Serve with dressing made of oil and lemon juice and salt.

TURNIP SLAW SALAD

3 cups grated turnip
1 onion grated
1 head of lettuce
2 tablespoons olive oil
1 tablespoon wine
  vinegar
Coarse salt and coarse
  black pepper, as
  desired

Vitamin C for the preservation of small blood vessels. Calcium and Vitamin D as well, for bones and teeth.

Mix turnip and onion, season to taste with salt, pepper, oil and wine vinegar. Arrange on lettuce cups.

RAW CAULIFLOWER SALAD

2 cups sliced raw cauli-
  flower or in flowerets
1 onion, chopped
3 stalks of celery with
  leaves
1 head of lettuce
½ teaspoon coarse salt
⅛ teaspoon red crushed
  pepper

A and C helpful in healing wounds. Good for skin and eyes.

2 tablespoons olive oil
2 tablespoons wine
  vinegar

Mix the vegetables with oil, vinegar and seasonings. Place on shredded lettuce and serve chilled.

STRING BEAN SALAD

¼ lb. raw green or yel-
  low string beans
  (may be pickled)
1 green pepper
1 mild onion
1 head of lettuce,
  shredded
4 tablespoons olive oil
3 tablespoons wine
  vinegar
½ teaspoon coarse salt
¼ teaspoon coarse
  black pepper

Contains elements which provide chemical balance in the blood. Rich in calcium and phosphorus necessary for pregnant women. Aids in building bones and teeth.

Cut the string beans into ½ inch pieces, or you may mince them. Cut up onion and green pepper, with the seeds. Blend all the vegetables with oil, vinegar and seasonings to taste.

TURNIP AND CARROT SLAW

2 cups turnips, grated
1½ cups carrots, grated
¼ teaspoon coarse salt
2 tablespoons olive oil
2 tablespoons lemon or lime juice
⅛ teaspoon red crushed pepper

The Vitamin A content in carrots is converted in the body as a pro-vitamin. Turnips with their C vitamin, calcium, and phosphorus cooperate to keep blood vessels firm.

Mix the grated turnips, carrots and blend with the seasonings and one or two tablespoons of oil. Use lemon juice or wine vinegar.

COLESLAW

3 cups shredded or grated cabbage
1 small onion, grated
¼ teaspoon coarse salt
½ teaspoon celery seeds
¼ teaspoon mustard seeds
2 tablespoons olive or peanut oil
2 tablespoons lemon juice or wine vinegar

Cabbage and lemon juice, power ful in ascorbic acid, help to prevent hemorrhages in the circulatory system. Vitamin C guards the small blood vessels. The skin retains its natural moisture with the A content here. The iron value in green vegetables and nut oil help to prevent anemia.

1 carrot, shredded
⅛ teaspoon red crushed
   pepper

Blend all ingredients and chill. For variation, add ½ cup of pimiento and ½ cup of chopped green pepper. The addition of one whole egg further enhances the flavor of coleslaw.

WHITE RADISH SLAW

3 large white radishes,
   grated
1 tablespoon lemon juice   *More Vitamins C, A and B, in*
   or wine vinegar   *order of quantity, in radishes.*
2 tablespoons olive, corn
   or peanut oil
Coarse salt and pepper,
   as desired

Blend together all ingredients and chill. Add grated onion if desired.

RAW LIMA, PEAS AND CARROT SALAD

1 cup raw baby lima
   beans, fresh
1 cup raw green peas   *These are carbohydrates for food*
1 cup shredded carrots   *energy, growth, and development.*

SALADS

1 small Bermuda onion,
  minced
2 tablespoons olive oil
1 tablespoon lemon juice
  or wine vinegar
Coarse salt and pepper,
  as desired

High in Vitamin A, calcium, phosphorus, and Vitamin D.

Combine lima beans, peas, and carrots with onion and blend with oil, lemon juice and seasonings to taste. You may grind up the beans and peas, if desired.

CUCUMBER SALAD

3 large cucumbers,
  sliced thin
1 large Bermuda or red
  onion
1 teaspoon olive oil
2 tablespoons wine
  vinegar
Coarse salt and coarse
  black pepper, as de-
  sired

Excellent C source. Do not peel, since vitamin is found on outside layer of cucumber. Keeps gums in good condition, heals and keeps small blood vessels strong. Needed for bones and teeth.

Do not peel, but penetrate the skins with a fork lengthwise. Dice onion. Blend with condiments and dressing. Serve chilled, as a relish or as a salad on shredded lettuce.

CUCUMBERS IN SOUR CREAM

2 large cucumbers,
   sliced
2 scallions, minced
1 stalk of celery, cut up
2 cups sour cream
Coarse salt and coarse
   black pepper, as de-
   sired

Biotin, which is found in ferments and yeast, aids in preventing thinness in hair, gray in hair, and hunching of back. Helpful in overcoming lassitude, dermatitis, and somnolence.

Combine ingredients and serve chilled. Pot cheese and red radishes may be added to this salad.

OLIVE-ONION DELICACY

2 cups green or black
   olives, sliced thin
1 cup onions, sliced thin
3 tablespoons olive oil

Rich in oils and minerals.

Combine and serve on shredded lettuce, or as a relish.

STUFFED AVOCADO

2 avocado pears, cut in
   halves
3 teaspoons grated
   onion

A good substitute for meat, and even more easily digested. May

1 stalk celery, chopped fine

Coarse salt and coarse black pepper, as desired

1 tablespoon lemon juice or wine vinegar

help maintain chloresterol balance.

Scoop out halves of avocado. Mash avocado meat with onion, celery, salt, pepper and lemon juice or wine vinegar and stuff back into avocado shells. Serve chilled.

AVOCADO PEAR SALAD

2 avocados, cut in halves

Lettuce, shredded

1 tablespoon lemon or lime juice

Same as above.

Coarse salt and coarse black pepper, as desired

Place avocados on lettuce and season.

AVOCADO AND TOMATO SALAD

1 avocado, diced

2 stalks celery,

chopped
3 fresh tomatoes
¼ teaspoon grated
onion
1 tablespoon olive oil
Coarse salt and red
crushed pepper,
as desired
1 teaspoon wine
vinegar

Avocado in combination with to-mato offers even more resources for minerals.

Combine the vegetables and add oil, vinegar and seasonings.

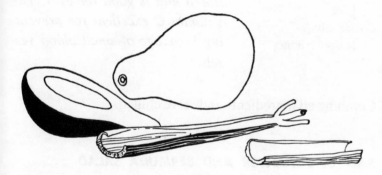

AVOCADO IN CELERY STALKS

2 avocadoes, mashed
¼ onion, grated
½ lemon or lime, juiced
3 celery stalks
Coarse salt and coarse
black pepper, as desired

Mineral salts in celery aid in good bone, muscle and nerve tissue.

123

Combine the avocado meat with onion, lemon juice and seasonings to taste. Stuff into celery.

CABBAGE AND PINEAPPLE SLAW

1 head cabbage, grated (3 cups)
½ cup grated or shredded fresh pineapple
1 tablespoon olive oil
2 teaspoons lemon juice
Coarse salt
1 teaspoon honey

Vitamin A plus here with cabbage and pineapple. Full of carotene that can be converted by body into a pro-vitamin. Can be stored and is good for eyes. The Vitamin C excellent for preventing breakage of small blood vessels.

Combine all ingredients and serve chilled.

RAW CAULIFLOWER AND BERMUDA SALAD

1 head raw cauliflower, cut into flowerets
1 medium Bermuda onion, diced
½ cup Provolone cheese
½ cup large green olives
1 head crisp lettuce
3 tablespoons olive oil

As a raw food, no worry about fragile C vitamin disappearing. Just wash, do not peel cauliflower so the outside layer can remain full of Vitamin C.

124

2 tablespoons lemon
     juice or wine vinegar
Coarse salt and coarse
     black pepper, as de-
     sired

Wash cauliflower and separate into flowerets. Dice onion, cheese, and olives. Combine all four foods with oil, lemon juice or vinegar and seasoning to taste. Chill and serve on shredded lettuce.

STUFFED TOMATOES

4 large fresh tomatoes
½ cup chopped celery
¼ cup onion chopped
1 cup grated raw
     potato
½ cup chopped cucum-
     ber
1 can of anchovies
1 tablespoon olive oil
1 tablespoon wine
     vinegar
Head of lettuce, shredded
Coarse salt and red
     crushed pepper,
     as desired
Dash oregano
Basil leaf

A blend of Vitamins A, B and C plus necessary mineral salts.

Cut off tops of tomatoes and scoop out. Mix the scooped out tomato meat with other vegetables, the anchovies, and combine with oil, wine vinegar and seasonings. Stuff into tomato shells and serve chilled on shredded lettuce.

STUFFED RAW GREEN PEPPERS

4 green peppers
2 fresh tomatoes, mashed
½ cup chopped celery
¼ cup chopped onion
½ cup chopped cucumber
1 head lettuce
1 cup wild rice soaked overnight (water is absorbed by rice, so no loss)
4 slices of raw lean bacon
3 tablespoons olive oil
2 tablespoons wine vinegar
Coarse salt and red crushed pepper, as desired

The eyes have it! A special value of Vitamin A. Low in calories.

Wash the green peppers and scoop them out. Mix the seeds with the mashed tomatoes, chopped celery, onion, cucumber and combine with wild rice. The rice should be

126

mixed with the finely chopped bacon. Mix all with oil, vinegar and seasonings. Stuff into the chilled green pepper shells and serve on lettuce. Note: If a white rice is preferred, use the Italian Avorio Rice which, soaked overnight, is easy to prepare in this way. This rice can be bought in a Health Food Store or in an Italian shop.

TROPICAL WALDORF SALAD

1 cup cubed unpeeled apples
1 cup cubed fresh pineapple
1 cup chopped celery
½ cup chopped un-sulphured dates
½ cup chopped un-sulphured figs
½ cup raw chopped nuts
½ cup raw pumpkin seeds
1 tablespoon olive or peanut oil
1 tablespoon lemon juice
3 tablespoons honey
⅛ teaspoon coarse salt
1 head of lettuce

This varied assortment lends itself well to a balanced blend of Vitamins A, B and C plus important minerals. Good as a meal or a snack—vitamin rich and calorie low.

Combine all the fruits with lemon juice and honey and oil (if desired) and salt. Serve chilled with lettuce leaves.

127

RAW BACON SALAD

6 strips raw lean bacon
   or Canadian bacon
1 small red hot pepper
2 cups diced unpeeled
   apples
1 cup chopped celery
1 scallion, chopped
1 tablespoon lemon
   juice
Coarse salt, if desired

Fast tissue builder full of phosphorus. The B vitamins here hasten enzyme reaction.

Combine all ingredients with seasonings. Serve chilled on lettuce.

APPLE SALAD

2 large apples
2 cups red or white
   grapes
1 cup chopped walnuts
½ cup fresh orange
   juice
2 tablespoons honey
1 tablespoon lemon or
   lime juice
1 head Romaine
   lettuce

A is for apple and also for Vitamin A. The eyes can shine and the skin tissues can be bright.

Mix lime or lemon juice with honey, combine with fruits and nuts. Serve chilled on lettuce.

128

ASSORTED FRUIT SALAD

2 bananas, sliced
1 cup diced apple with
   peels
1 cup diced plums
1 cup pitted halved red
   cherries
3 tablespoons lemon
   juice
2 tablespoons honey
½ cup sliced peaches
½ cup sliced pears
1 orange, sectioned
½ grapefruit, sectioned

The natural sugars here are good "pepper uppers" and provide the vital elements for body repair and vitality.

Combine all of the fruits with lemon juice and honey, which should be mixed beforehand. Chill and serve on lettuce. If you wish, you may sprinkle some nuts or pumpkin seeds over the salad.

APPLE AND BANANA COMBINE

2 cups grated apple
3 bananas, mashed
½ cup orange juice
2 tablespoons honey
1 tablespoon lemon
   juice
1 head lettuce

No, bananas are not fattening. (Only 88 calories!) And so rich in A, B, C vitamins and in minerals that the calories are used by the body and not put on as fat.

129

It makes a perfect noon meal or snack. Eyes and skin benefit from the Vitamin A in the apple.

Combine fruits with lemon juice and honey, which should be mixed beforehand. Chill and serve on lettuce.

APPLE SLAW

2 cups apple, grated with peel
2 cups red cabbage, shredded
½ cups diced celery
2 tablespoons lemon juice
2 tablespoons honey
Lettuce leaves

Build up your alkaline reserve and mineral salts. Apple is easily digested this way and perfect for the infant, or aged with a chewing problem. Eyes can glisten and be bright and skin can be colorful and healthy with Vitamins A and C.

Combine all ingredients. Chill and serve on lettuce.

SKY BLUE PINK SALAD

2 red apples, diced with peels
2 oranges
½ grapefruit

Energizing and rich in iron and calcium—a blood builder.

1 cup grapes
1 cup honeydew,
   watermelon, and
   cantaloupe balls
2 bananas, sliced
1 peach, sliced
1 pear, sliced
2 tablespoons honey
2 tablespoons lemon
   or lime juice
Romaine lettuce leaves

Section and cut oranges and grapefruit. Wash and halve grapes, removing seeds. Cut up bananas and chill in orange or lemon juice. Combine all other fruits with lemon juice and honey, mixed. Chill and serve arranged on lettuce leaves.

FRESH FRUIT CUP

1 cup diced oranges
½ cup diced grapefruit
2 bananas, sliced
1 cup diced fresh pine-
   apple
½ cup melon balls
½ peach, sliced
½ pear, sliced
2 tablespoons honey
2 tablespoons lemon
   juice
½ cup nut meats

The Vitamin C in the citrus fruits keeps small blood vessels strong and firm. A tasty path to vim, vigor, and well-being.

131

Combine all the fruits with mixture of lemon juice and honey. Sprinkle with nuts. Chill and serve in sherbet glasses.

ROSEBUD SALAD

1 head lettuce
1 grapefruit
1 orange
1 banana
1 cup watermelon, honeydew, canta- loupe balls
1 mango or fresh peach
1 cup nut meats
Few dried dates, unsul- phured
Few fresh or dried figs, unsulphured
¼ cup raisins
½ cup dried rose petals
2 tablespoons honey
2 tablespoons lemon juice

The unusual here. Rose petals are scattered over this not only for decor, but for taste and flavor. Naturally all the vitamins and minerals are snug in the lettuce nest.

Mix the honey with lemon juice and combine with all of the fruits and nuts. Chill and serve on lettuce cups. Scatter the rose petals over each.

BLUEBERRY DELIGHT

2 cups fresh blueberries
1 cup fresh melon balls
1 cup fresh cottage
cheese
3 tablespoons honey
1 tablespoon lemon juice

The A here is extremely high, so protect the eyes and eye membranes with this delicious berry.

Mix berries with honey and lemon juice. Place mound of cheese in center of fruit plate on bed of lettuce leaves. Surround the cheese with berries, and the melon balls.

FRESH STRAWBERRY ICE FEAST

1 box fresh strawber-
ries (2 cups)
1 pkg. Knox plain gela-
tin
½ cup honey
1 teaspoon lime or
lemon juice
½ cup warm water
2 oranges, sectioned
1 grapefruit, sectioned
1 or 2 bananas, sliced
1 cup watermelon balls
1 cup cantaloupe balls
1 cup sun-dried, unsul-
phured dates

Calories low and health high!

☞

1 cup sun-dried, unsul-
   phured figs
1 cup chopped walnuts,
   pecans or/and
   almonds
Coarse salt, as desired

Edge circular platter with crisp lettuce on which grape-fruit and orange sections are placed. Make next inner ring of sliced bananas; the next one of watermelon and canta-loupe balls; the next one sliced peaches, and in the center of the platter place scoops of the strawberry ice. Garnish with figs, dates and nuts. The Ice: Mix gelatin with water, honey and lemon juice and combine with strawberries. Chill until jelled, firmly.

PINE-BERRY SALAD

1 cup diced fresh pine-
   apple
2 cups fresh strawberries   *More A here to add to the berries.*
1 sliced banana
2 tablespoons lemon
   juice
2 tablespoons honey
Lettuce leaves

Combine the fruits with juice and honey. Chill and serve on lettuce leaves.

RAISIN ORANGE SLAW

3 cups grated cabbage
1½ cups unsulphured
raisins
2 oranges sliced and
cut
2 tablespoons lemon
or lime juice
2 tablespoons honey

Herewith the high-phosphorus raisin.

Toss shredded cabbage with oranges and raisins mixed with orange or lemon juice and honey. Chill and serve.

STRAWBERRY-MINT SALAD

2 cups fresh strawber-
ries
½ cup fresh mint leaves
1 head lettuce
1 pkg. plain gelatin
½ cup honey
½ cup warm water
1 teaspoon lemon juice
Coarse salt, if desired

The oil and chlorophyll in mint leaves are just what one needs for a sweet breath.

Clean and cut strawberries, mix with mint leaves and combine with gelatin which is already mixed with water, honey, lemon juice and salt. Let stand until firmly set in refrigerator. Serve on lettuce or in sherbet glasses.

135

PEACH OR MANGO SALAD

2 mangoes, or peaches
1 mashed banana
1 head lettuce
3 tablespoons honey
2 tablespoons lemon
   juice
Berries, if desired

Exceedingly high A so paramount in care of eyes, teeth, nerves and muscles (especially mango).

Wash carefully, but do not peel all the skin from the mangoes or peaches, and slice. Combine with strawberries or blueberries mixed with honey and lemon juice. Chill and serve on lettuce or as fruit cup.

STRAWBERRY AND BANANA SALAD

2 cups strawberries,
   mashed
1 banana, mashed
1 head lettuce
2 tablespoons lemon or
   lime juice
4 tablespoons honey

Very nourishing and energizing. A real builder-upper.

Blend the strawberries and bananas with honey and juice. Serve chilled on lettuce with raw certified cream or grated coconut.

136

ORANGE AVOCADO STUFF

2 avocados, cut in
  halves
1 orange, diced
1 head lettuce
½ lemon rind, minced
1 teaspoon honey
Coarse salt, if desired
Romaine lettuce leaves

Abounds in A and in valuable vegetable fat and organic salts.

Dice avocados and together with orange pieces mixed with lemon rinds and honey, stuff into avocado shells. Place on Romaine lettuce leaves.

COCONUT SURPRISE

1 fresh coconut,
  grated
2 large apples, grated
  with skins
1 head lettuce
½ cup unsulphured rais-
  ins, dates or both
3 tablespoons honey
1 teaspoon lemon juice
Coarse salt, if desired

High in natural nut oil and in B vitamins. One of nature's most concentrated foods, good for bones and teeth. Easy to digest as a liquefied milk for infants, pregnant women and aged persons.

Stir together part of the coconut, all of the apple, and raisins or dates with honey and lemon juice; mold into balls, cover with shredded coconut and serve as such or on lettuce leaves.

CHEESE A LA PRUNES

½ lb. cottage cheese
   made of raw milk, if
   possible
½ lb. large prunes,
   soaked overnight
   (keep the juice)
1 cup of nut meats
1 tablespoon honey
1 teaspoon lemon juice
Coarse salt, if desired

A vitamin in prunes good for the eyes. Laxative and toning for intestinal tract. A good regulator.

Drain prunes, cut, blend with cheese and add nut meats. Serve on lettuce. The drained off liquid from prunes can be chilled and served as prune juice.

RAW PEANUT BUTTER ROLL SALAD

1 cup raw peanut butter
1 cup raw peanuts,
   crushed
2 cups grated carrots
2 tablespoons honey
Lettuce leaves

Pure body builder. So good for children, even infants when the combination is liquefied. Closest to mother's milk when honey and spring water is added to raw peanut butter.

Combine peanut butter with honey and salt and add to raw carrots. Mold into balls, roll in raw peanuts and serve on lettuce leaves.

MANGO HALVES

2 mangoes
1 banana, diced
1 head lettuce
1 cup berries (strawberries or blueberries)
2 tablespoons honey
1 teaspoon lemon juice

Rich in A vitamin necessary to all ages in care of eyes, teeth, nerves and muscles. Iron, calcium, phosphorus and Vitamin D perfect for mineral riches and balance in bone structure.

Slice mangoes in halves. Scoop out mango meat, leaving about ½ inch on the peel. Dice the mango meat and blend with bananas, berries and honey with lemon juice and salt. Serve chilled on lettuce.

PAPAYA SALAD

2 cups diced papaya
2 cups berries
1 head lettuce
1 banana sliced
3 tablespoons honey

The important Vitamin A again. Seeds of papaya a source of pepsin, so an aid to digestion. Helps

1 teaspoon lemon juice
Coarse salt, if desired

to neutralize gases in intestinal tract, a good regulator. Has a reputation in South American countries for improving male vigor.

Combine chunks of papaya, berries, sliced banana and honey with lemon juice and salt. Chill and serve on lettuce.

PEAR RING SALAD

2 pears, sliced length-
  wise
2 small bananas (or 1)
1 head lettuce
1 orange, sliced thin
1 cup strawberries
4 tablespoons honey
1 teaspoon lemon juice
Coarse salt, if desired

Full of mineral values good for building bones, teeth, nerves and muscles. Very effective as a laxative. Low in calories.

Arrange pears at outer rim of circular platter, then a row of bananas, and then one of the orange slices. Place the berries mixed with honey, lemon juice and salt in the center. Place all on shredded lettuce.

MELON CIRCLE SALAD

2 slices of watermelon
1 cantaloupe, cut in
   wedges
½ honeydew melon, cut
   in wedges
Lettuce

Excellent Vitamin A content and plentiful source of naturally distilled water. Good for kidneys. Low in calories, cooling to the body machine.

Cut with rinds all melons into wedge-like pieces and arrange alternately on shredded lettuce.

FRUIT CUP MELON RING SALAD

1 cantaloupe
1 banana, sliced
1 cup pitted black
   cherries
½ cup diced fresh pine-
   apple
3 tablespoons honey
1 teaspoon lemon or
   lime juice
Coarse salt, if desired

Abounding in A. The berries clean house.

Wash and cut cantaloupe into 1 inch width (sliced around to make circles) removing seeds and rind. Fill the melon slice center with the bananas, cherries, and pineapple which is mixed with honey, juice and salt. These fruits are to be chilled thoroughly before combining them into

141

such a salad. Add grated coconut, if desired.

TANGERINE SALAD

4 tangerines or
   mandarin oranges
1 banana
1 head lettuce, shredded
2 apples with skins
1 cup nut meats
4 tablespoons honey
1 teaspoon lemon juice
Coarse salt, if desired

Refreshing source of Vitamins A, B and C. Fruit sugar, for energy, is easily assimilated. Large amount of calcium, iron, and phosphorus.

Break tangerines into sections, add sliced bananas, diced apples, nuts, honey, lemon juice and salt. Toss together with crisp lettuce and serve.

STUFFED PRUNE SALAD

1 lb. prunes, soaked
   overnight (keep
   juice)
1 head lettuce
1 cup cottage cheese,
   made of raw certified
   milk, if possible
4 tablespoons raw cer-
   tified cream
½ cup chopped nuts

Impressive Vitamin A content in prunes, good for eyes. Very laxative. Cheese a nourishing protein.

Blend cream and cheese together. Pit prunes and stuff with cheese mixture and nuts. Serve in hearts of lettuce.

APRICOT-CHERRY CUP

4-6 fresh apricots
2 cups pitted black cherries
1 head lettuce
Fresh mint leaves
2 teaspoons lemon or lime juice
2 tablespoons honey
Coarse salt, if desired

Attractive, tasty, and energizing no-cook dish.

Blend diced apricots with skins, and pitted cherries. Stir in honey mixed with lemon juice and salt. Toss in the mint leaves. Chill and serve on lettuce or in sherbet glasses.

FRUIT JELLIED SALAD

1 cup diced orange
1 sliced banana
1 head lettuce
½ cup pitted black cherries
½ cup strawberries

Combined with gelatin, a good melange of vitamins and minerals. The gelatin is protein, good for nails, teeth and hair, but is

SALADS

1 pkg. plain gelatin
¼ cup orange juice
¼ cup warm water
4 tablespoons honey
1 teaspoon lemon juice
Coarse salt, if desired

only of such benefit when accompanied by fresh fruits.

Stir gelatin in warm water until diluted. Combine with orange juice, honey, lemon juice and salt. Stir in fruits and jell in the refrigerator. Serve on lettuce.

CANTALOUPE A LA CHEESE

1 or 2 cantaloupe, chilled
2 cups cottage cheese
3 tablespoons raw certified cream
1 cup pitted black cherries

Vitamin A again, to benefit eyes. Cheese has body building and repair value; is one of the best sources of protein.

Wash and cut the cantaloupes into 1 inch thick rings, removing seeds. Mix cheese with cream until smooth and fill cantaloupe rings. Garnish with cherries.

STUFFED FRESH PEAR HALVES

2 fresh pears, cut in halves

144

1 cup cottage cheese or
  sour cream
1 tablespoon honey
1 teaspoon lemon juice
1 cup chopped pecans
½ cup chopped unsul-
  phured black figs
Coarse salt

Cheese—a body building, and energy-giving food.

Thoroughly mix the cottage cheese with sour cream or with honey, lemon juice and pinch of coarse salt. Blend with figs and nuts, and stuff into pear halves. Garnish with fresh cherries.

FRESH SALMON ASPIC SALAD

3 cups salmon, shred-
  ded (seared slightly
  beforehand and
  cooled)
¼ cup diced green pep-
  per
¼ cup diced celery
3 tablespoons wine vin-
  egar
1 tablespoon lemon
  juice
1 cup chopped cucum-
  ber and onion

Sea minerals and Vitamin A in salmon tissue builders, very digestible and a fine source of protein. The gelatin is good for nails and a quick energy booster.

☞

SALADS

Coarse salt and red
    crushed pepper
 2 pkgs. plain gelatin
 1 cup warm water
 1 teaspoon honey
Watercress

Dissolve gelatin in warm water, add honey, salt, pepper, vinegar, and lemon juice. Chill until almost firm. Add the vegetables and the salmon. Jell until firm. Unmold and serve on watercress.

TOMATO ASPIC SALAD

 4 cups freshly made to-
    mato juice
 1 cup diced onion
 5 drops Tabasco
½ teaspoon lemon juice
¼ teaspoon coarse salt
 2 pkgs. plain gelatin
¼ cup warm water
 1 tablespoon wine vin-
    egar
 1 basil leaf
Dash oregano
Lettuce or watercress

Energy-giving vital mineral salts. The gelatin is a fast tissue builder.

Dissolve gelatin in warm water. To tomato juice add Tabasco, salt, onion, basil leaf, oregano, wine vinegar, lemon juice and other seasonings. Chill until firm. Un-mold and serve on lettuce or watercress.

SMOKED HAM SALAD

2 cups diced smoked
  ham
1 onion, cut up fine
2 stalks celery
1 cup diced Provolone
  cheese
1 teaspoon English dry
  mustard
1 tablespoon olive, corn
  or peanut oil
Hearts of lettuce

Real he-man food as body building protein. The added zest of celery and condiments make it a good-tasting salad.

Combine smoked ham, cheese, onion and celery. Add the mustard paste (made of dry mustard, oil and salt) and serve on lettuce. Cheese may be omitted, if desired.

HAM-NOODLE SALAD

1 cup diced raw
  smoked ham
2 cups noodles,* pre-
  pared beforehand
1 head lettuce
1 onion, grated

Again a man's dish—high in protein and carbohydrates.

147

SALADS

½ cup raw green peas
½ cup diced celery
 1 tablespoon olive oil
Coarse salt and crushed
   red pepper

*Preparation of noodles:

1 pkg. noodles, semolina
   and spring water type
4 cups water heated hot
   (not boiled) with salt
   (1 or 2 tablespoons)

Leave noodles in hot water and salt for about five minutes then cool. Combine ham, noodles, peas and celery with oil and seasonings. Chill and serve on lettuce or water-cress.

VEGETABLE MACARONI SALAD

½ cup raw green peas
½ cup diced celery
 1 onion, grated
½ cup raw grated car-
   rots
 2 cups elbow macaroni
   (semolina type) pre-
   pared as indicated
   above for noodles in
   Ham and Noodle
   Salad

A fine mixture of vitamins in such gay array. Such combinations miss very few, if any, of necessary elements for the perfect meal.

2 tablespoons olive oil
Coarse salt and red
    crushed pepper, as
    desired
1 head lettuce, shred-
    ded

Combine vegetables and macaroni with oil and season-ings. Chill and serve on shredded lettuce.

CHEESE SALAD

1 cup Ricotta cheese
1 cup grated Romano
    Italian cheese
2 tablespoons grated
    onion, or 1 scallion
    chopped fine
1 head lettuce, shredded
2 tablespoons raw sour
    cream
Coarse salt and coarse
    black pepper, as
    desired

A good protein substitute for meat. Refreshing with vegetables which add the vitamins and minerals necessary for good health.

Combine cheeses with onion and sour cream. Season. Chill and serve on shredded lettuce.

149

MACARONI OR NOODLE SALAD

3 cups macaroni or
  noodles*
1 scallion, chopped
1 cup Provolone and
  Parmesan, grated
  (cheese)
4 cups olive oil
Coarse salt and pepper

Rich in carbohydrates and minerals, mainly phosphorus, good for bones and muscles. The cheese, as protein, healthy for body repair and building as well as energy. High B vitamin content.

Mix thoroughly the macaroni, cheese, onion, oil and seasonings. Chill and serve on lettuce, Romaine is suggested.

CRAB OR SHRIMP SALAD

2 cups flaked crab or
  shredded shrimp
  (prepared by searing
  fast and cooling)
1 head lettuce, shredded
½ cup diced celery
½ cup sliced green
  olives
1 scallion chopped

Low calorie combination rich in Vitamins A and C. Good for skin, eyes and small blood vessels. Shellfish are high in iodine content, important for mineral balance.

* Macaroni or noodles prepared as indicated in recipe for noodles in Ham and Noodle salad.

2 tablespoons olive oil
¼ teaspoon coarse salt
¼ teaspoon red crushed
    pepper

Combine crab or shrimp, olives, celery and onion with oil and seasonings and serve on lettuce.

JELLIED CRAB OR SHRIMP SALAD

1 pkg. plain gelatin
1 cup warm water
3 tablespoons wine vin-
    egar
½ teaspoon salt, coarse
    or sea
2 cups crab meat or
    shrimp (seared
    quickly and cooled)
½ cup celery diced
2 tablespoons olive,
    corn or peanut oil
½ cup sliced olives
1 head lettuce,
    shredded

The added element of gelatin provides a bit more protein and makes a cool dish for supper on a hot night. Solo or duet these two shellfish help fill iodine needs of the body and Vitamins A and B.

Dissolve gelatin in water. Add seasonings, oil, vinegar, celery, crab or shrimp and olives. Chill and serve on lettuce.

151

SMOKED WHITEFISH SALAD

2 cups smoked whitefish,
  shredded
1 cup diced celery
4 tablespoons grated
  onion
1 cup diced cucumber
1 tablespoon olive, corn
  or peanut oil
1 tablespoon lemon or
  lime juice
1 head lettuce, shredded

The oil in whitefish aids in growth, better skin, good kidney function. The process of smoking helps to retain more vitamins and minerals than cooking.

Combine the fish, celery, onion and cucumber with oil, lemon juice and seasonings. Chill and serve on lettuce. (May make this aspic.)

HORSERADISH MOLD SALAD

½ cup grated fresh
  horseradish
1 pkg. plain gelatin
2 cups warm water or
  juiced fresh red beets
  (juice in electric
  blender)
Wine vinegar, to taste

A most piquant dish in result as well.

Dissolve the gelatin in water or beet juice. Add the horseradish and some wine vinegar.

152

ANCHOVY SALAD

1 head of lettuce, quartered
1 can anchovies (flat fillets in olive oil)
Olive oil to taste
Wine vinegar to taste
6 black olives

Here is another fish presented in a more perfect process, i.e., salted and preserved in olive oil. The value of the fish oil is again in aiding growth, skin and reproductive function. The added vitamins and minerals in lettuce and olives are of high protein value.

Arrange anchovies and olives on lettuce. Season with oil and vinegar, mixed.

CHOPPED EGGPLANT MOLD

3 cups chopped raw eggplant
1 scallion, chopped
2 tablespoons wine vinegar or lemon juice
1 stalk celery, chopped
1 tablespoon olive, corn or peanut oil
Coarse salt and black pepper, as desired
1 head lettuce, shredded

Mineral high and calorie low! What a tasty relish to relish and help to regain mineral values for the body bones and blood.

153

Blend eggplant, onion, celery with oil, vinegar and seasonings. Chill and serve alone or on crisp lettuce.

RAW BACON AND TOMATO SALAD

1 cup raw lean bacon or
   Canadian bacon
4 tomatoes   *Bacon very high in phosphorus.*
1 stalk of celery
1 scallion
Basil leaf
1 head lettuce, shredded

Mix together the bacon, tomatoes, cut up in sections, diced celery and the onion slices. Chill and serve on lettuce. If desired, omit onion.

ESCAROLE SALAD

1 head escarole, cut into   *The Vitamin A wealth in this let-*
   pieces   *tuce can be stored in the body to*
Olive oil   *make certain that the eyes are*
Wine vinegar or lemon   *kept in good condition.*
   juice
Coarse salt

Toss escarole with wine vinegar, oil, garlic and coarse salt.

ESCAROLE AND RADISH SALAD

1 head of escarole, cut into pieces
1 cup red radishes, sliced
½ cup sliced black or green olives
1 tablespoon olive oil
1 tablespoon wine vinegar
½ teaspoon coarse salt

The combined Vitamin A plus B and C of radishes set forth the alphabetic vitamin needs of the body. The energy results abound.

Toss escarole with radishes, olives, oil and vinegar, and salt. Chill crisp and serve.

SMOKED TONGUE SALAD

2 cups diced smoked tongue, raw
1 small onion or scallion, cut
1 stalk of celery, cut
2 tomatoes, cut into pieces
1 head lettuce, shredded
2 tablespoons olive oil (mixed with mustard below)

The minerals and Vitamin B make tongue of value for bones and teeth. As a protein it is a fast tissue builder.

155

1 teaspoon hot dry
  English mustard
¼ teaspoon coarse salt

Mix tongue, onion, celery and tomatoes with oil, mustard and salt. Serve chilled on shredded lettuce.

CELERY STUFFED WITH SMOKED LIVERWURST

1 bunch Pascal celery
¼ lb. smoked liverwurst
¼ teaspoon dry mustard
8 green olives

Tasty liverwurst contains an enormous quantity of Vitamin A, excellent for the care of the eyes and eye membranes. The bones and teeth are well provided for in the excellent mineral content in the meat. The mineral salts in celery are considered good for the nerves.

Mix liverwurst and mustard thoroughly, stuff into stalks of celery and serve on lettuce. Garnish with olives.

SMOKED PASTRAMI SALAD

2 cups smoked pas-
  trami, sliced (raw
  Italian type)

Pastrami is rich in Vitamin B,

1 small onion, cut
1 stalk of celery, cut
¼ cucumber, pickled, chopped
¼ cup green peppers and green tomatoes, pickled, chopped
1 head lettuce, shredded
Olive oil to taste, if desired

phosphorus, and calcium, necessary for good bones and teeth, blood and muscle tissue. Salad contains Vitamin A and C.

Combine diced pastrami, onion, celery, pickled cucumber, pepper and tomatoes, and serve on shredded lettuce.

ITALIAN TYPE SAUSAGE SALAD

1 air-dried hot, mild or sweet sausage, diced
3 fresh tomatoes
1 head Romaine lettuce, escarole, or endive
1 tablespoon olive oil
½ tablespoon wine vinegar

The calcium, phosphorus and fat herein aid in building good bones, teeth, and skin. The protectors in Vitamins A, B, and C are found again in the tomato and lettuce.

Rub garlic in bowl, mix sausage, Romaine cut up, olive oil and vinegar, salt to taste, and garnish with quartered tomatoes on shredded lettuce.

157

SMOKED CHICKEN OR DUCK SALAD

2 cups diced chicken or
   duck, smoked
2 stalks of celery, cut up
1 red onion, sliced for
   garnish
1 head iceberg lettuce
Olive oil
Lemon or lime juice
Coarse salt and black
   pepper, as desired

Protein in chicken or duck for fast tissue building. Celery and other salad vegetables add the A and C vitamins otherwise missing.

Mix chicken or duck, celery, and lettuce with oil, lemon juice, and salt and pepper. Chill and serve on cupped lettuce. Garnish with sliced red onion.

SMOKED PORK SHOULDER SALAD

2 cups smoked pork
   shoulder, diced
2 cups celery, diced
1 onion, diced
2 tablespoons olive oil
2 tablespoons lemon
   juice
¼ teaspoon coarse salt
1 teaspoon dry English
   mustard, mixed with
   water
1 head lettuce,
   shredded

A happy combination of meat with the salad vegetables.

Blend oil, lime or lemon juice, salt and mustard paste, and combine with pork shoulder, celery and onion. Serve on lettuce.

PROSCIUTTO OR RAW SMOKED HAM SALAD

1½ cups raw ham or
    Prosciutto, diced
 ½ cup chopped pickle
 2 stalks of celery,
    chopped
 1 red onion, sliced
    for garnish
 2 teaspoons dry
    mustard
 2 tablespoons wine
    vinegar
 ¼ tablespoon coarse
    salt
 1 head Romaine let-
    tuce

Smoked ham retains much of its B vitamins and minerals such as calcium, phosphorus and iron so needed for good bones, teeth, and health.

Combine diced meat with pickles, celery, mustard and seasoning. Serve on lettuce and garnish with onion and parsley.

PICKLED HERRING SALAD

2 cups pickled herring,
   sliced

☞

SALADS

1 cup raw onion rings
2 hearts lettuce
8 green olives

Like meat, fish serves as an abundant source of protein and is, therefore, a fast tissue builder. It is also a piquant appetizer.

Arrange herring on lettuce with onion, green olive and cream, if desired.

SMOKED HERRING SALAD

4 strips of smoked herring
2 raw onions, sliced in rings
2 hearts lettuce
8 green or black olives
1 bunch of celery hearts
1 tablespoon olive oil
1 tablespoon lemon juice

The fat content in fish, such as herring, is important for growth, good clear, smooth, moist skin, good kidneys, and healthy reproductive functions. The calcium, phosphorus, and iron reserve here results in good teeth and bones. Vitamin A maintains the eyes.

LENTIL SALAD

2 cups lentils, soaked in water and 2 tablespoons coarse salt for 48 hours. (Change water four times.)
1 cup raw carrots, cut fine

Lentils are high in mineral values and good for the building of body, bones and teeth. Vitamin A is high here, so that the eyes are well provided for. The addition of

1 cup raw fresh green
   peas
3 tablespoons olive or
   peanut oil
Coarse salt and coarse
   black pepper, as
   desired
½ cup grated onion
1 head lettuce,
   shredded

salad vegetables make the dish full of Vitamins A, B and C.

Combine lentils, carrots, peas and onions with oil and seasonings. Chill and serve on shredded lettuce.

COLD BEAN SALAD

2 cups red kidney
   beans, fava or navy
   beans (soaked for 48
   hours)
1 onion, chopped fine
4 fresh tomatoes,
   mashed
2 stalks of celery, diced
1 green pepper,
   chopped
⅛ teaspoon oregano
¼ teaspoon coarse salt
2 tablespoons olive oil
2 crisp hearts of lettuce

High mineral and vitamin content are added in the vegetables. Beans have high protein value, but are apt to be gas forming, so use judgment in serving.

Mix together beans, onions, tomatoes, celery, green pepper, oil and seasonings. Serve chilled in cupped lettuce.

161

RED AND GREEN TOMATO SALAD

4 fresh ripe tomatoes, quartered and sliced
2 pickled green tomatoes
1 onion, chopped fine
1 stalk of celery, chopped
1 head lettuce
Olive, corn or peanut oil
Coarse salt and red crushed pepper, as desired

Eliminates toxins because of its vital mineral salts content.

Combine all vegetables with oil and seasonings. Chill and serve in cupped lettuce.

162

5. MEATS AND FISH

Meats and fish are high in proteins, so they are active in building healthy body tissues. This is especially true when they are prepared with a minimum of heat and most certainly when they are eaten raw. E.g. "Steak Tartar."

BEEF STEAK

Beef steak (rib, porter-
   house, sirloin, club,
   etc.)
Coarse salt and pepper
Garlic

Animal proteins are good as quick boosters to prevent anemia. They are fast energy sources. The body can manufacture its fats and carbohydrates out of pro-

☞

teins. With its amino-acids, meat is a complete protein. Since every part of the body requires protein in some quantity, it is important to add protein as a tissue builder and repairer.

Broil or pan sear, rare. (1 or 2 minutes on each side.)

GROUND BEEF PATTIES (HAMBURGERS)

1 lb. ground beef,
chuck, or shin meat
½ teaspoon coarse salt
¼ teaspoon red
crushed pepper
1 raw egg
1 small onion, chopped

The meat should be ground only one time, in order to retain as much blood as possible. Season and add egg, and broil or pan sear for a minute on each side on very hot skillet. Serve raw as "Steak Tartar."

CHICKEN BROILERS

Cut the chicken at each joint, season with salt, pepper, garlic, oregano and sear rapidly on hot pan or broil on high. Use Soya sauce as seasoning if desired.
Chicken may be used with vegetables or rice or noodles.

CORNED BEEF OR PROSCIUTTO

These types of beef can be used as bought without further preparation unless one wishes to have them warm. When warming, cut into slices and sauté in pan very quickly over high heat.

SMOKED BEEF TONGUE

This can be used as bought without further preparation unless one wishes it warm. Slice and warm quickly over low heat.

DRIED BEEF

Shred beef and soak in warm water and drain. Add seasonings as desired and heat slightly with oil, or butter. If creamed use certified raw milk, but heat only very slightly. (2 minutes)

SMOKED HAM

Prepare the ham with or without the pineapple, honey and cloves. Use hot oven to begin with, turn to 200° and let stay in for five minutes, then without heat for 15 minutes. Before serving broil for two minutes.

LIVER

Calf, beef, pork, lamb or chicken livers may be used. The most valuable of these is pork. Then in value are: chicken, beef, lamb and last of all calf. Sauté or broil very quickly in a small amount of oil over a very hot heat. (About 1 to 2 minutes.)

KIDNEYS, HEART OR SWEETBREADS

A rich source of vitamins and minerals. Quick blood builder. Sauté in oil over high heat for about 2 minutes.

BARBECUED SPARE RIBS

Cut meat into individual ribs. Season and broil or barbecue over open coals close to flame for 1 to 3 minutes. Serve immediately with hot mustard.

VEAL (SHOULDER, LEG, RUMP, ETC.)

Cut into 1½ inch slices and either broil or pan sear as indicated for beef.

LAMB

Same as for veal. May also be ground as hamburg.

PEPPERONI

Italian type red pepperoni, dried sausage or sweet dried sausage. Slice thin and serve raw since it is smoked or air-dried. Warm if you wish, very quickly on pan on high heat. (Less than a minute.)

166

FISH DELIGHT

4 fillets, or steaks (1"
  thick)
Crawfish
Lobster
Shrimp
Oysters
Clams
etc.
2 tablespoons peanut oil
  or butter
2 tablespoons chopped
  parsley
Coarse salt and pepper,
  as desired

Broil or pan sear in oil (no longer than 1 minute on each side). Season and cover. Melt the butter, combine with parsley or chives and pour over the fish with some lemon wedges or juice of lemon or lime.

6. CEREALS

OLD-FASHIONED OATMEAL

1 cup raw oatmeal
1 cup warm water
1 tablespoon coarse salt

In cereal form, oats possess an abundance of elements that build blood, help the nerves and give energy and stamina.

Add the salt to the oatmeal while in the water and soak overnight, or for an hour. Warm to taste over low heat, stirring constantly. Serve with honey, certified raw milk or light cream or coconut milk and some fresh fruit in season. One may also add raisins or other dried fruits.

WHOLE WHEAT CEREAL

1 cup raw whole wheat
1 cup warm water
1 teaspoon coarse salt

A source of needed minerals and vitamins is found in all seeds. All add to the foundation, building and repair of the bone and muscle structure of the body.

Soak overnight or for an hour. Warm to taste over low heat, stirring constantly. Serve with milk, cream or coconut milk and fresh or dried fruits, as desired.

UNTOASTED CREAM OF WHEAT

1 cup raw cream of
  wheat
1 cup water
1 teaspoon coarse salt

The infant and aged needs assuaged here in this easily digested cereal. When prepared this way, all the minerals and vitamins remain for body growth, repair and energy.

Soak the cereal overnight and warm to taste over low heat, stirring constantly until ready to eat. Serve with honey, milk and fresh or dried fruits, as desired.

CORN MEAL

2 cups yellow corn
meal
1½ cups water
1 teaspoon coarse salt

The incomplete protein in the corn is made complete by the added milk or cream.

Soak overnight or for an hour or two. Warm to taste over low heat and stir constantly (1 minute). Serve with fresh or dried fruit, milk, cream or coconut milk and honey.

Quick supper dishes in cereal form can be prepared as above. They can be made into pancakes, or loaves. Sear them over low heat in butter or oil. Tan them, do not brown them! This may be served with butter and salt, and with or without milk.

Some people like to make them into cupcakes or muffins by putting them into muffin tins and in the oven (200°) to air dry for about five minutes with heat on, and fifteen with heat off. Good with salads as a quick supper or with some meat or fish.

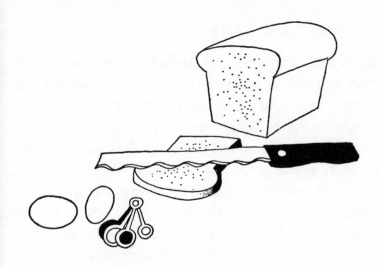

7. BREADS AND CAKES
DON'T BAKE—AIR-DRY

WHOLE WHEAT BREAD

½ cup whole certified
   raw milk
3 cups whole wheat
   flour
2 tablespoons honey
1 teaspoon coarse salt
1½ tablespoons olive or
   peanut oil
1 cake or package of
   yeast
½ cup water

The thiamine B in wheat and richness in yeast are heavy in whole wheat bread. The husks remain and contribute towards building a good nervous system and a strong heart.

173

Warm milk, add honey, salt and oil. Combine water with yeast and add to first mixture. Add flour gradually and using a little flour on board, knead into a smooth firm dough. Pat into ball-like shape and place in a greased bowl. Cover with a cloth and let the dough rise again to double its bulk. Knead again and divide into two equal parts; brush the dough with a little oil so that a crust will not form, and let it rise again. Fold the dough again, and shape into small loaves. Let rise again, put into oven with temperature at 150 to 200° for five minutes. AIR-DRY for 20 minutes with heat off. (Heat oven beforehand, very hot.) The bread may remain in oven for an hour, or until ready to serve.

WHEAT AND CORNMEAL BREAD

Same as above in procedure. With this substitution: (for 3 cups wheat flour)
2 cups whole wheat flour
1 cup cornmeal or corn flour

The incompleteness of corn is taken care of with the whole wheat. Another true staff of life.

OATMEAL BREAD

2 cups old-fashioned oatmeal

1 cup whole wheat flour
¼ cup warm water
1 pkg. yeast
½ cup certified raw milk
2 teaspoons coarse salt
4 tablespoons honey
2 tablespoons olive or peanut oil

The minerals and starch of porridge are all here. As a cereal, oats are the most nutritious. Oats are also noted for their contribution towards an improvement of the nervous system. As such, they can be considered a natural sedative.

Use the same procedure for preparing the dough as for the whole wheat bread with the substitution of oats for whole wheat. Temperature 150-200°

. . . . 20 minutes with heat off
5 minutes with heat on

Start with very hot oven.
Turn heat off and leave bread in oven 60 minutes.

RYE BREAD

Same ingredients as above, but substitute flour:
4 cups whole rye flour

Ranks high in protein.

Same procedure as for breads indicated in previous recipes.

CORN BREAD

4 cups certified raw
milk
1½ cups cornmeal
½ teaspoon coarse salt
1 tablespoon olive,
corn, or peanut oil
4 beaten eggs

More Vitamins A, B and C in this bread than in oats or rye. The incompleteness of corn as a protein is overcome by use of milk and eggs.

Soak cornmeal in milk for about an hour. Add salt, oil and eggs. Pour into well-greased pan and place in very hot oven for about 5 minutes, then for 5 minutes in 200° oven and finally leave in for 45 minutes with heat turned off.

ENGLISH MUFFINS

1 cup certified raw
milk
3 tablespoons peanut
or corn oil
½ teaspoon coarse salt
2-3 tablespoons honey
1 package of yeast
1 egg, beaten
3½ cups whole wheat
flour
1 cup cornmeal

In the yeast (true of all these breads) is found the best source of Vitamin B, since it stores up vitamins. Bread that is exposed to sunlight has the added Vitamin D.

176

Combine milk with oil, honey, salt and yeast already dissolved in water. Add egg and flour. Beat until well combined. Then, stirring in the remaining flour, knead on the floured board until dough is elastic. Place in a greased bowl for about an hour or two or until double in bulk. Punch down and roll dough out on floured board to ¾ inch thickness. Cut into circular cookie shapes, 4 inches wide in diameter and place on a cookie sheet sprinkled with cornmeal. Cover with wax paper and allow to rise in a warm place until double their size in bulk. Turn and sprinkle with remaining cornmeal. AIR-DRY in low heat on an ungreased pan until slightly tanned on both sides. (3-5 minutes)

WHOLE BRAN BREAD

1½ cups whole bran
1 cup certified raw milk
1 egg
3 tablespoons olive or peanut oil
½ cup whole wheat flour
2 tablespoons honey
½ teaspoon coarse salt

The calcium and phosphorus so needed in building bone, teeth and body tissue prevail here. The stimulation of bran for regulating the elimination function is not to be overlooked. Cleansing the body is primary as a requisite for good health.

Let bran and milk stand for 3 minutes together. Add beaten egg, oil, honey and salt. Then combine the wheat flour with the bran mixture. In greased pan place in oven and leave for 5 minutes, then 30 minutes, with heat off. May be in longer.

All of these breads may be made into "muffins" by being "air-dried" in regular muffin tins. Place these in oven with heat on for five minutes and then with heat off for ten minutes. The same amount of heat as for the breads.

WHOLE WHEAT PANCAKES

2 cups whole wheat
  flour

1 cup certified raw milk
  (sweet or sour)

1 egg

2 tablespoons olive,
  corn or peanut oil

2 tablespoons honey

½ teaspoon salt,
  coarse or sea

Contains minerals that can assist in body and bone growth. The Thiamine, as often added to bread, is basically and naturally here in whole wheat. Important for nervous system and healthy heart.

Combine honey, egg, salt and oil, and stir slowly into flour alternating with milk. Drop by spoonfuls on griddle over very low heat. Turn over when consistent enough and let dry thoroughly.

WHOLE WHEAT AND CORNMEAL PANCAKES

Use same ingredients as
above with this substitu-
tion:
1 cup whole wheat flour
1 cup corn meal

The higher Vitamin A content in cornmeal adds vitamin vigor to this cake.

Follow same procedure as for Whole Wheat Pancakes
below.

OATMEAL PANCAKES

Use above recipe, sub-
stituting 1 cup of old-
fashioned oatmeal for
cornmeal

Provides nourishing elements which produce energy and endurance. Good for nerves.

WHOLE WHEAT WAFFLES

  2 cups whole wheat
    flour
  1 cup certified raw milk   *Full of Thiamine.*
  2 eggs
½ teaspoon coarse salt
  2 teaspoons peanut,
    corn or olive oil
  2 tablespoons honey

179

Combine honey, eggs, salt and oil. Add the flour slowly, alternating with the milk. Place in hot waffle iron. When of proper consistency and only slightly tanned, serve.

WHOLE WHEAT AND CORNMEAL WAFFLES

Same ingredients as above with this substitution:

1 cup whole wheat flour
1 cup cornmeal

The strong combination of cereals with their respective vitamins and minerals appeal to both the eye and the taste buds.

Follow procedure for waffles above.

FRESH FRUIT WAFFLES

1 cup fresh blueberries
1 cup fresh blackberries
1 cup bananas
1 cup fresh chopped
   pineapple
1 cup strawberries

A nutritious treat.

Any or combinations of these fruits may be used in the batter of the whole wheat waffle recipe.

DRIED FRUITS OR NUT WAFFLES

1 cup raisins
1 cup dates
1 cup figs   *More concentrated vitamins are*
1 cup pecans, walnuts,   *added here.*
  almonds, raw peanuts,
  etc.

Any or combinations of these may be used in the batter
of the whole wheat waffle recipe.

WAFFLES TOPPED WITH FRESH FRUITS

Any one of the fresh
fruits in season may be
used as a topping for   *The fruits make the waffles a*
WHOLE WHEAT   *more complete source of body*
WAFFLES and other   *building elements.*
waffles. This can serve as
a dessert or a light lunch
or a supper.

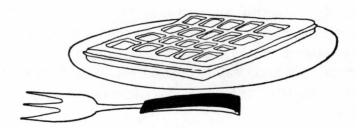

MAVILYA FRUIT CAKE

2 cups chopped dried
  figs, unsulphured
2 cups chopped dried
  dates, unsulphured
2 cups chopped pecans
2 cups grated almonds,
  used like flour
¼ cup honey
1 cup dried apricots,
  unsulphured
1 cup dried peaches
1 cup raisins
1 cup currants
1 orange rind, ground
  up
1 lemon or lime rind,
  ground up
Juice of orange and
  lemon
2 tablespoons wine or
  rum or brandy

Delicious in taste. A most perfect wedding cake, a complete sweet for the body. Energy!

All of the dried fruits may be ground up in a meat grinder. Blend ingredients together as smoothly as possible, and then place in a mold or squares on wax paper in the refrigerator until firm. Roll in crushed nuts. Slice with a wet knife and serve with whipped certified raw cream, if desired.

182

FRUIT COOKIES AND BROWNIES

- 2 cups chopped dried figs, unsulphured
- 2 cups chopped dried dates, unsulphured
- 2 cups chopped pecans or any other nut
- 1 cup freshly grated coconut
- 1 cup grated almonds, used like flour

Minerals and vitamins put into a form that both children and adults can enjoy.

183

¼ cup honey
1 cup dried apricots or/
   and peaches,
   chopped
1 cup raisins
½ teaspoon lemon juice
1 teaspoon salt, coarse
   or salt from sea

Blend all these ingredients together except nut and coconut, and mold into cookie shapes or squares. Then roll in crushed nuts or coconut.

To make the brownie, add some pure cocoa (Swiss or Dutch) and more honey.

COCONUT DATE SWEETS

2 cups grated coconut
1 lb. unsulphured dates,
   pitted
1 cup almonds or pecans

Rich in protein, sugar and carbohydrates and most palatable. All contribute towards body building and a higher energy level.

Place an almond into each date. Roll it in coconut. Wrap each piece individually in wax paper and put into refrigerator. Serve.

184

COCONUT OLD HAVANA SURPRISE

1 cup freshly grated
  coconut
4 egg whites, beaten
½ cup honey
1 tablespoon whole
  wheat or rice flour

Such a rare combination for a sweet tooth! Energy plus for the body.

Mix together and air-dry in oven pre-heated hot. Then turn to 200° and let remain for five minutes with heat on. Then turn off heat and permit to remain for 15 to 20 more minutes.

8. DESSERTS

Fruits in season make the most delicious desserts. Some of the recipes listed under APPETIZERS can be served as a dessert. E.g.:

Minty Orange
  and Grapefruit
  Surprise
Fruit Cup
Banana Cocktail
Melon Balls in
  Sauterne Wine
Fresh Peaches in
  Port Wine
Berry-Mint
  Cocktail
Canteloupe and
  Banana Half

The perfect balance in vitamins and minerals that round out the diet of the human being. Contributes to the health of body, mind and spirit.

DESSERTS

APRICOT OR PRUNE WHIP

2 cups dried apricots or
 prunes
½ cup honey
1 teaspoon lemon juice
2 egg whites, beaten
½ cup whipped certified
 cream

When used for corrective purposes, extremely good for constipation disorders.

Blend all ingredients except cream with a hand beater or an electric blender. Chill and serve with light cream.

GRAPEFRUIT A LA HONEY

Grapefruit, cut in halves
Honey

The citrus provides mineral and mineral salts to cleanse the system, and kidneys in particular.

Remove seeds and core grapefruit. Top with honey. Brown (lightly) in broiler using high flame.

BANANA, APPLE, BLUEBERRY YUM

2 cups washed blueber-
 ries
3 teaspoons honey
2 mashed bananas
1 grated apple with skins

Berries are very effective in the treatment of constipation and skin difficulties (teen agers).

Blend bananas, apples and honey, over which you pour blueberries. May use electric blender. Top with certified whipped cream, if desired.

PINEAPPLE COCONUT DESSERT

2 cups diced fresh pine-
apple
1 cup shredded fresh
coconut
3 teaspoons Sauterne or
Malaga wine blended
with 2 teaspoons
honey

A body builder, good for treating anemia.

Pour wine and honey over pineapple and chill. Sprinkle with fresh coconut before serving.

STRAWBERRIES 'N' CREAM

2 cups strawberries
4 tablespoons honey
½ cup certified raw
cream or sour cream

Like all berries, strawberries are rich in iron.

Chill the berries and honey. Serve with cream. May be varied with combinations such as banana, pineapple, other berries and nuts.

189

DESSERTS

CHERRIES RUM

2 cups black or red cher-
ries, pitted
4 teaspoons honey
1 cup certified raw
cream, whipped
1 tablespoon rum

Like the above for berries. The rum, for added stimulation.

Combine all and pour rum over. May light it, if you wish.

RHUBARB

2 cups fresh rhubarb,
chopped fine, or li-
quefied in an electric
blender
½ teaspoon lemon juice
Honey

Good for quick energy.

Combine honey with lemon and mix with rhubarb. If desired, warm slightly over low flame for few seconds.

MANGO FLIP

2 cups mashed mango
pulp
1 cup chopped pecans
1 cup whipped raw
certified cream

Good source of natural sugar and iodine.

190

Whip the cream with the mango and then add the nuts.
Chill and serve. For variation, sprinkle with coconut,
shredded.

ICE CREAM

3 cups certified raw
   cream, whipped
3 eggs
½ teaspoon coarse salt
½ cup honey
1½ cups certified raw
   milk
1 pkg. plain gelatin
1 teaspoon vanilla
1 cup fresh fruit

*The great American favorite. Can
be made the proper and health-
giving way, to present protein and
animal fat to the body!*

Warm milk slightly, and mix into the gelatin, vanilla,
honey and salt. Remove from heat, cool, and add whipped
eggs and cream. Place in freezer for about an hour and
then mix in the fruits. A good rum or wine may be
used for flavor.

FRESH FRUIT "JELLO"

1 envelope plain gelatin
½ cup warm water
½ cup fruit juice
    or
½ cup honey
⅛ teaspoon coarse salt

*Gelatin lacks vitamins and miner-
als, so add the fruits. Good for
nails and skin.*

191

Gelatin and water or juice should be thoroughly mixed. Add the fruits or nuts after it has jelled for about 20 minutes. Add bananas, berries, nuts, dates, figs and/or other fruits.

9. NO-COOK
QUICK SUPPER DISHES

MACARONI, NOODLES AND SPAGHETTI

1 lb. semolina type
  macaroni, noodles or
  spaghetti
4 cups hot, but not
  boiling, water
3 tablespoons coarse salt
2 tablespoons olive oil

A child's favorite. Fixed "al dente" it can provide much of the vitamins and minerals required for protection of body needs for growth and function.

Place the noodles, spaghetti or macaroni into hot water with salt and oil, and let stand for about five minutes.

ITALIAN SPAGHETTI

½ lb. semolina type
   spaghetti, Italian type
   excellent
2 cups very hot water
2 teaspoons coarse salt
   and fresh red pepper
6 tomatoes, liquefied
1 chopped onion or 1
   scallion
1 diced green pepper
1 stalk celery with
   leaves, chopped
1 clove garlic

*The vegetables enrich this dish
with their respective vitamins and
minerals especially Vitamin C in
tomatoes.*

Prepare the spaghetti as indicated in recipe for spaghetti.
Sear quickly over high heat on film of oil, tomatoes, garlic
clove, onion, pepper and celery. Add the seasonings and
olive oil. Meat balls may be added.

SPAGHETTI WITH CHICKEN

1 fresh young broiler,
   cut at each joint
3 teaspoons peanut,
   corn or olive oil
Dash oregano
Basil leaves
2 cloves garlic, minced
Coarse salt and crushed
   red pepper as desired

A fun and protein combo.

Prepare the spaghetti as indicated in recipe above. Heat pan containing a film of oil and the garlic. Remove garlic when it is browned and sauté the chicken which will be seasoned later with salt, pepper, oregano and basil leaves. Turn them over in 3 minutes and leave for another 2 minutes. Cover and remove from fire and serve immediately.

NOODLE CHOP SUEY

1 pkg. noodles
1 chopped onion or
  scallion
1 green pepper, chopped
2 stalks celery with
  leaves, chopped
1 cup chopped fresh
  mushrooms
3 tablespoons olive oil
2 fresh tomatoes,
  mashed
2 teaspoons cornmeal
Dash oregano
Basil leaf
Bay leaf
Coarse salt and crushed
  red pepper

Confucius say the best of noodly dishes.

Sauté the vegetables over high flame (1 minute). Add the cornmeal. Remove from flame and add the mushrooms. Place the noodles, which are already prepared in manner described in first recipe, with the vegetables and serve.

WILD RICE

1 cup wild rice, soaked
   overnight
2 cups hot water   *In its own rich coating, rice is*
2 teaspoons coarse salt *especially wealthy in minerals.*

Warm rice, which has soaked up the water, and serve with milk, butter or oil. This particular dish with all the vegetables including fresh mushrooms and seasoned with coarse salt and crushed red pepper and some Soya sauce is always a great favorite. It can be combined with chicken, pork or beef.

Fried rice is made with this rice or an Italian white rice (Avorio Rice) and mixed with seared scallions and a raw egg.

10. MID-NITE SNICK-SNACKS

Don't go to bed hungry, just eat the right thing.

FRUITS

Banana	*Dates*
Apple	*Figs*
Pear	*Tangerines*
Orange	*Mango*

MID-NITE SNICK-SNACKS

Grapefruit
Grapes
Watermelon
Honeydew

Raisins
Dried Peaches
Dried Apricots
Fresh Apricots

CHEESE AND FRUITS

Apple slices and pear slices with aged cheeses such as:

Gorgonzola
Camembert
Cheddar
Swiss
Roquefort
Bleu Cheese

Cut the fruit into round slices, and fill the holes with a bit of cheese.

CUCUMBER SURPRISES

Slice cucumber thin and spread with:

Raw peanut butter
Raw cashew nut butter
Cheese
Crushed nuts and currants
Caviar

OATMEAL MIX

Mix oatmeal with fruits of any kind and a little milk or none, as desired. May use dried fruit.

Also, use cut up tomatoes with raw oatmeal, oil and seasonings. (Coarse salt, pepper, and oregano or basil leaf)

A kind of Pizza:

> 1 cup raw oatmeal
> 2 tomatoes, liquefied in blender
> ½ cup Cheddar or Provolone cheese
> 2 tablespoons olive oil
> Coarse salt and dash of oregano

Mix together and heat in a pan until hot.

TEA OR COFFEE

Use Peppermint tea

If iced coffee desired, use one cup of hot coffee with 6 chunks of ice and put into blender. Mix thoroughly. It will taste and look like it had all the fixings in it. Very foamy.

INDEX

202

203